Creating a
COURTYARD GARDEN

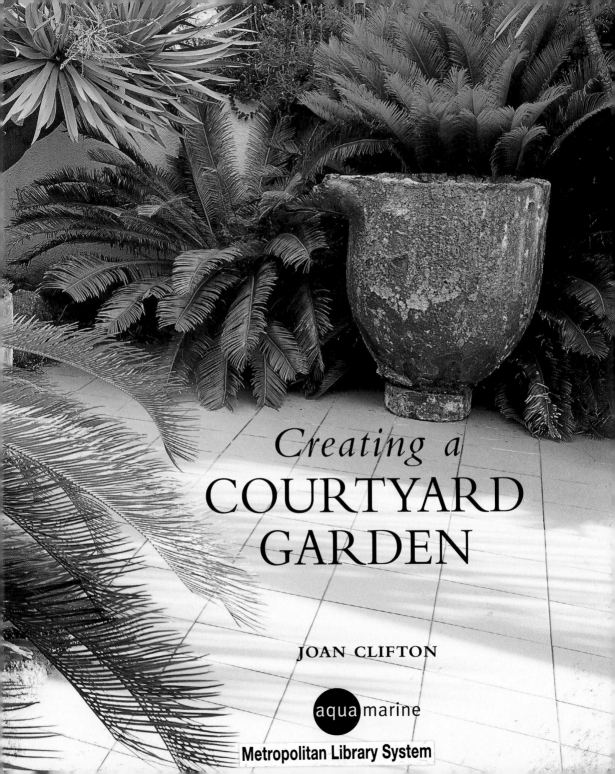

Creating a
COURTYARD
GARDEN

JOAN CLIFTON

aqua marine

This edition is published by Aquamarine,
an imprint of Anness Publishing Ltd,
Blaby Road, Wigston,
Leicestershire LE18 4SE;
info@anness.com

www.aquamarinebooks.com; www.annesspublishing.com

If you like the images in this book and would like to investigate
using them for publishing, promotions or advertising, please visit our
website www.practicalpictures.com for more information.

Publisher: Joanna Lorenz
Managing Editor: Judith Simons
Executive Editor: Caroline Davison
Senior Art Manager: Clare Reynolds
Designer: Louise Clements
Illustrator: Rob Highton

PUBLISHER'S NOTE
Although the advice and information in this book are believed to
be accurate and true at the time of going to press, neither the
authors nor the publisher can accept any legal responsibility or
liability for any errors or omissions that may have been made nor
for any inaccuracies nor for any loss, harm or injury that comes
about from following instructions or advice in this book.

contents

INTRODUCTION

The courtyard, which for centuries has
been a significant feature of domestic
architecture, is seeing a reincarnation in the
small gardens and roof terraces of today.
An area enclosed by four surrounding walls
and entered through a gateway, it originally
formed the entrance to the house, a place for
residents to create a secure haven. Today,
it encompasses terraces and patios as well as
enclosed courtyard spaces.

The ancient Egyptians first developed the idea of a courtyard garden at least 5,000 years ago, creating lush oases that gave some protection from the harsh desert environment beyond the walls. As life became more civilized, courtyards developed in sophistication, especially in hotter regions, to become areas of repose and relaxation, filled with shady palm trees and cooling fountains. Formal in style, with a paved or cobbled floor, the courtyard was contained within the house (or palace), with windows opening internally on to it, and hidden from public view.

The style of courtyards may have developed over the centuries, but they have remained as popular as ever. The modern courtyard adopts the concept of containment within boundaries, but is now likely to comprise the entire outdoor space. It is an exceptionally effective treatment for a small garden, especially in a constricted urban environment, encompassing privacy, seclusion and romantic illusion. Its economy of scale allows the user to invest in high-quality landscaping and special effects, with lavish planting that is encouraged by a microclimate in which tender subjects can be cultivated.

In Japan, where building space is at a very high premium, the courtyard concept has become a design philosophy in its own right, incorporating the "viewing garden" – a miniature landscape seen from the house through doors or windows or from a viewing terrace.

In this book, we focus on courtyard designs to suit different lifestyles. Looking at the garden space from the point of view of the user, we cover five contrasting looks, including smart courtyards, courtyards for entertaining, country-style courtyards, contemplative spaces and contemporary design, with a practical case study in each section. We examine the key elements, whether these are sculpture and ornament, furniture, or water features, that are suitable for each style to help you develop a personal look for your own courtyard.

Containment and seclusion are the essence of a courtyard garden, with boundary walls and fences providing both a decorative backdrop for an intimate stage set and a screen from neighbours or an undesirable view. Boundaries should be high enough to provide seclusion, turning the focus upon the internal composition, but not so high as to form a claustrophobic barrier that would make the area seem small and oppressive. Walls should constitute part of the design and can be used to create illusory special effects: *trompe l'oeil* treillage can help the space to appear large; mirror panels bring in reflected light and suggest a

secondary space; while painted murals introduce a sense of fantasy. Trellis, a good vehicle for those all-important climbing plants, may be applied as a decorative facing or to raise the height of walls or fences.

The incorporation of three-dimensional design is especially important in a contained space, to add both visual interest and perspective. Changes of level, using devices such as steps and terraces, raised planting beds and above-ground pools, will transform a flat plot into a series of interesting spaces, while, at ground level, paths create both the spatial dividing lines and the links, playing a role in directing movement to provide a sense of mystery and discovery.

above right *The small scale of these stable paving setts suits the intimacy of this city terrace. The occupants are assured of privacy and seclusion by a densely enclosing screen of evergreen foliage.*
opposite *Oversized terracotta planters give an impression of scale and presence to this classical Italianate courtyard.*
previous page *Clipped topiary lends a smart formality to this courtyard garden, with its unusual garden furniture.*

The hard landscaping, which includes the floors and boundaries, can often become a controlling element in a courtyard design if a balance with the planting is not maintained. The finish of built structures affects the appearance of the courtyard, and it is important to recognize the characteristics of different types of stone, metal and wood before undertaking any work. A wide choice of textures exists, with finishes varying between polished and reflective, smooth and matt, or rough and rugged, even within one type of stone. The choice can alter the ambience and style of the design. It is a complex and costly part of the design process, with durability and suitability for purpose also to be taken into account. For this reason, a section of the book focuses on materials for ground surfaces, boundaries and built structures, as well as different finishes.

The physical structures within a courtyard act as a framework to support the planting, which constitutes the soft elements of the design. In their way, plants demonstrate similarly varied characteristics to hard landscaping materials, having qualities of texture and form that range from the strong and dynamic to the soft and gentle. Try to recognize the planting styles that will fit comfortably into the scene you are trying to achieve.

Water adds an extra dimension, and can also be used to create different moods. A wildlife pond bordered by reeds and flowering irises introduces calm and tranquillity, while a cascade tumbling into a pool brings noise and excitement. Classical formality, organic subtlety and technical innovation can each have a place in the courtyard scenario. Water is a seductive element, so let yourself be tempted. A hot tub spa or gurgling rill, a carp pond or a swimming pool – the style and scale are determined only by your desires, and your budget.

For most of us, the courtyard is a place to relax and unwind, somewhere to invite friends and spend time with the family, all of which demand a comfortable place for sitting and eating. Finding the appropriate furniture can be quite a task, however, because it must contribute positively to the design of the courtyard while being practical enough to adapt to differing social demands. If this were not enough of a challenge, it also has to be able to withstand the ravages of sun and rain, unless you have space for out-of-season storage. With so many examples of shapes and materials, from solid teak armchairs to lightweight aluminium loungers, and price tickets ranging from the affordable to the very pricey, it is worth taking a little extra time to choose a design that will give you lasting pleasure and service.

A contained space offers plenty of scope for dramatic effect, and a carefully designed lighting scheme can turn a placid, daytime courtyard into a theatre of focus and shadow at night.

above Pots of pretty flowers and a rusticated finish soften a flight of steps in this sun-soaked Mediterranean courtyard.
right Low walls, capped with old terracotta tiles, form a textural screen around this Mediterranean courtyard. The soft, mellow finish provides a subtle background for the planting of smooth, spherical topiary as well as spiky yuccas and phormiums.

A sculpture or fountain will shimmer out of the gloom and trees make silhouettes around the walls, while a terrace can be transformed into an intimate dining area with hanging lanterns and tiny spotlights.

Atmosphere can be created in a number of other ways, and sculpture is increasingly appreciated for its sympathetic role within a natural environment. The choice of style is utterly subjective, of course, with some people preferring familiar figurative forms while others opt for the abstract or daring. Sculpture serves many purposes: it can provide amusement, surprise or even shock. It will always be a talking point, but, perhaps most importantly, it should also become a favourite possession to be cherished and admired.

Dramatic effect needs focus and concentration to be successful, and a single bold feature will not only give your design character and interest but can also seem to make the space feel larger. It can be as much of a visual mistake to dot lots of small objects around as to plant one each of a huge number of different plants.

Container planting can also play a sculptural role, particularly if you use a single large container as a focal point, with a suitably dramatic plant. Alternatively, create the effect of a bed by grouping a number of containers together. An informal, yet still unified, effect can be achieved by using containers of different shapes and sizes, but all in a similar colour or material. Alternatively, with pots in a variety of styles and materials, use the colours and textures of the planting scheme to link them harmoniously.

The choice of plants for the containers is, of course, subjective. Evergreens and succulents can be co-ordinated in form and texture to create a cool, modern look that lasts all year. This is helpful if you want a low-maintenance courtyard. Alternatively, to change the scene throughout the year, why not indulge in a confection of fruits, flowers and heady scents, with a different colour theme for each change of season?

above *A serene marble fountain, set upon a plinth of immaculately detailed mosaic, dominates this Islamic-style courtyard. It is planted with roses and colourful herbs that evoke the design of an exotic carpet.*
opposite *On a hilltop perch, the walls of this courtyard are softened by a dense clothing of white-flowered climbers. The walls enclose a vibrant pool and spa, clad in a modern mosaic of brilliant blue and turquoise, while a pair of mop-head figs stand guard at the door.*

A smart sanctuary has a distinctive look and ambience, being composed of clean, formal lines and symmetrical structures and filled with fine specimen plants, elegant ornaments and decorative features. Such a formally designed courtyard can also have an atmosphere of great serenity and calm, and the limited space available in a courtyard lends itself to this formal approach. A large formal garden may be prohibitively expensive to create, with quantities of statuary and large containers, and is also likely to require a lot of work to keep it looking good. So, if you like the idea of a formal garden that is more easily achieved, a courtyard space is the answer.

smart

SANCTUARIES

A smart formal courtyard can fulfil a special need for discerning gardeners, enabling them to create a significant and mature garden, but on a thoroughly manageable scale. It may be a dedicated space within an existing rural garden or it may be part of a larger town plot. The smart sanctuary contains areas for relaxing and entertaining, while also providing the scope to indulge a particular interest, whether this is specimen plants, elegant containers or works of art.

The hard landscaping is the structural mainstay of the smart sanctuary and its success will depend entirely upon the quality of the design and the workmanship. Without this strong fundamental structure, the subsequent soft landscaping, or planting, will not be completely successful, which is, of course, the *raison d'etre* of the

courtyard. To achieve the sanctuary of your dreams, it is wise to consult a garden designer. A designer's relationship with suppliers puts him or her in a position to source the finest materials and find fabulous specimen trees and shrubs.

Not only will the formal courtyard provide a distinctive backdrop for specimen plants, but it will also act as the perfect gallery space for displaying works of art and sculpture. If you want to include some handmade art or craft works, then visit garden sculpture galleries and garden exhibitions in order to discover the wonderful work made by modern artists that will bring a whole new dimension to your sanctuary. If money is no object, commission a symbolic piece of contemporary sculpture, or perhaps an exquisitely handcrafted bench, to make your personal imprint on your private space.

opposite *A pair of terracotta urns makes a statuesque statement among the dramatic and exotic planting.*
below *Scale and simplicity inform this new classical design; the smooth pale finish of the hard landscaping is punctuated solely by the architectural planting in the raised beds.*
previous page *High walls, festooned with climbers such as bright pink bougainvillea, enclose this elegant courtyard.*

hard landscaping

above *Sawn sandstone paving reflects the tone and texture of the brick wall; the infill of beach gravel softens the overall effect.*

opposite *Changes of level introduce interest to a long narrow site. A rectilinear design of paving slabs accentuates the shape, while the snaking lines of the canal and the low retaining wall help to relieve its severity.*

The hard landscaping of a courtyard encompasses the main structural features of the design, including the floors and surfaces, boundaries and screens, and architectural features such as pools, flights of steps and raised beds. It forms a blank canvas on to which the other details of the courtyard, such as the furniture, water features, containers and even the planting, are imposed. Transforming just a small area of the garden means that the available budget can be spread generously, allowing the use of high-quality materials and the incorporation of special effects. To create an intelligent, elegant and well-executed design, you should take into account the architectural qualities of the house, research the character of the surrounding landscape, and develop the courtyard's full potential by an effective use of three-dimensional space and an imaginative application of resources.

Texture is perhaps one of the most important elements in the hard landscaping of a courtyard.

The hard landscaping, as well as additional decorative structures such as pergolas and gazebos, must be practical and reflect the users' needs. A bold, economical design is clean and visually pleasing, and especially suited to a location with space limitations, so avoid the temptation to build superfluous, distracting features.

The hard surfaces, which can be made from materials such as wood, brick and stone, can be further emphasized by cleverly contrasting finishes and colours. When considering the overall effect, bear in mind that highly polished surfaces can be tiring and aggressively formal, while, in general, textured finishes have a subtler character that is easier on the eye and more in tune with the natural qualities of foliage and stems.

The physical qualities of building materials are especially gratifying when employed in a sensory role; for example, solid wooden steps provide a reassuring ascent at the end of a crunchy slate walk, while linear borders of black marble, edging a path of pale flags, enforce the route and invite you to explore. This balance of soft and hard, dark and light, can be used to create dramatic or subtle effects, both visual and tactile.

above *Two square insets of dark paviors draw the attention to a change of level in the centre of a terrace and also bring visual relief to the elegant paving of smoothly sawn pale granite.*
left *Aggregates can transform concrete into a stylish and versatile paving material. A textured dark gravel finish is contrasted here with smooth white squares in order to produce a distinctive, diagonal, chequerboard design. This graphic layout also brings into sharp focus the sitting area within this intimate enclosure of creeper-clad walls.*

decorative features

Not every site is amenable to the changing of physical levels that can be created using flights of steps or raised beds, but that does not mean that the effect of a three-dimensional space need be lost. As an alternative to costly earthworks, architectural structures such as trelliswork, pergolas, arbours and gazebos provide a decorative solution and one that is of special interest to lovers of climbing plants.

The smart sanctuary is the ideal setting for a scheme of custom-made trelliswork to form the boundaries. Particularly suited to courtyards with existing high walls, an intricate design of fine wood mesh, worked to fit the scale and dimensions of the site, can elevate a plain rectangular space to the level of palace grandeur. It is especially useful for disguising an ugly or uninspiring wall. Panels of trellis are also valuable for creating height and privacy above a low boundary or concealing an undesirable view. By incorporating the visual device of *trompe l'oeil*, an illusion of distance can be created; the addition of mirror glass panels allows a sense of a secondary space.

Where a more naturalistic look is desired, the severity of courtyard walls or fences will certainly be enhanced by a clothing of textural foliage. Plant self-clinging species like Boston ivy (*Parthenocissus tricuspidata*), richly verdant in summer and radiant with fiery tints in autumn, or audaciously rampant

above *Bright steel spirals contrast with a dark zinc planter and lend support to climbing* Muehlenbeckia.
left *Arbours create shade in summer and provide excellent supports for cascading climbers such as this fragrant pink* Wisteria sinensis *'Amethyst'.*
right *A chic gazebo-like portico caps the centre of this intimate courtyard. Creepers and architectural shrubs are packed densely around the walls.*

trumpet vine (*Campsis radicans*), with its showering cascades of huge orange bells. Twiners and scramblers cannot manage to climb on their own and need extra help and support. The simplest and cleanest looking way to achieve this is by tying in shoots to horizontal wires set at 30cm (12in) intervals, and tensioned between special eye bolts fixed to the wall or fence posts.

The pergola is a versatile device that has been employed in courtyard gardens for many centuries. The Romans liked to create shaded walkways with it, while early illustrated manuscripts show how latticed structures were used to support grape vines in medieval courtyards. At its simplest, the pergola can be erected as a freestanding, cross-barred structure that is formed from wooden posts and rails, ranging in scale from a single arch framing an entrance to a complete covered walkway. This flexibility of design means that a pergola can be introduced into any size of courtyard.

Pergolas can be constructed from wood, iron or a cast aggregate (a material made from cement mixed with sand, gravel or crushed stone). The Art Deco period and Arts and Crafts movement provide excellent sources of inspiration for the bold, simple forms best suited to working in wood and reference to spatial arches in Japanese garden design can be equally rewarding for wooden structures.

In contrast, sanctuaries with a neoclassical theme demand the presence of elegantly proportioned columns to support the overhead structure, a fashion well represented by reproductions formed from cast aggregates. This style requires planting of appropriate grandeur, and wisteria, with its trailing racemes of soft lilac blooms, comes immediately to mind as the twiner best able to rise to the occasion.

When the appearance of visual lightness is required, forged iron makes an excellent construction material. Its combination of inherent physical strength and total flexibility allows it to be formed into complex designs. This might be a particular consideration if a romantic theme – perhaps of fragrant roses climbing over ornate metalwork – is desired.

With only a small change in specification, the pergola can also be adapted to become an attractive arbour. By omitting the supports on one side, extending the horizontal rails in length and attaching them to a building by means of a support rail bolted firmly into the wall, it becomes a private enclosure for an outdoor dining terrace.

The ultimate in decorative garden structures, however, must surely be the gazebo; always romantic, it may be forged from a confection of metal stems and spirals or be wooden-framed and enclosed with panels of intricate mesh. Whatever the design, it will make a show-stopping focal point especially suited to tumbling swathes of roses.

It should be borne in mind that climbing plants become exceedingly heavy with age, and the physical exposure of vertical structures makes them highly susceptible to wind pressure. The main proviso when building pergolas, arbours and gazebos, therefore, is that they should be very strongly constructed from stout materials, with the upright supports bedded firmly into the ground with concrete.

Where space for such features is unavailable, use an obelisk to introduce height into your courtyard. It can be used singly as a focal point or placed in formal groupings, perhaps set at the corners of a parterre. A pair of classically proportioned obelisks might frame a formal entrance door or provide emphasis at the start of a pathway. The obelisk may also be interpreted in a sinuously spiral form that is suited to the fluidity of an organic terrace design and especially useful for providing height and focus in a low bed. Flowers will push through the framework to the light, making a prominent show all over its surface. Large-flowering climbers are especially suitable, so for eye-catching effects try an effervescent passion flower (*Passiflora caerulea* 'Constance Elliot' is a seductively elegant white form) or any one of the colourful, larger-flowered clematis.

When placed in a square, painted wood, Versailles-style container, the classical obelisk makes a fitting stand-alone feature, best planted with an evergreen to give year-round performance. Ivy in one of its many forms is the obvious choice, but, more interestingly, star jasmine (*Trachelospermum jasminoides*) has the rare bonus for an evergreen climber of bearing scented, star-like, white flowers in late summer.

opposite *The immense form of this colonnaded arbour frames the fabulous sea view beyond. In keeping with the scale of the arbour, a large, yellow-flowered tree has been trained carefully at the outer edge to break the otherwise severe angularity.*
left *Massive steel circles form an original take on the planted tunnel; the slightly diagonal setting relieves their visual weight and leads the eye toward a group of slanted, circular, sculptural forms.*

classic containers

above left *Overflowing hyacinths and muscari follow the curvaceous form of this classical vase.*

above centre *Delicate spires of lily-of-the-valley (*Convallaria majalis*) relieve the severe style of this lead planter.*

above right *A generous terracotta oil jar bursts with trailing pelargonium and lobelia, with agapanthus to follow later in the season.*

Choosing the right plant for the right container is essential if you want to create an eye-catching result. It is a question not only of shape and proportion but also of taking into account the intrinsic characteristics of the pot and the plant. A Tuscan terracotta lemon pot, for example, will look more at ease when teamed with a grey-leaved Mediterranean olive (*Olea europaea*) or a dense clipped box tree than it would if planted with a spikily exotic New Zealand phormium or South American yucca. These plants demand slicker styles, such as a tall, straight-sided container, perhaps made from shiny metal or black-glazed stoneware. On the other hand, a gently bulging water jar from Thailand seems made for a quivering water grass, such as cyperus, or a slender bamboo.

Terracotta is a natural choice for a container because, being porous, it enables the soil to dry out naturally all over its surface, allowing the necessary balance in the potting mix between water and air. If your garden suffers from winter frosts, choose frost-proof pots, which have been fired at a minimum temperature of 1,000°C (1,830°F). Handmade pots stand out in appearance dramatically from machine-made products, and, if money is no object, you could import the best terracotta pots in the world from Impruneta, a tiny region in Italy. Both quality and design are superb, the pots are totally frost-proof and, as they weather, they look better with every passing year.

Stoneware containers make handsome alternatives – especially when created by an artist employing sophisticated textural and firing techniques. The main technical difference between stoneware and terracotta is the former's lack of porosity, which makes stoneware pots extremely resistant to weathering; normally frost-proof, stoneware's appearance will remain virtually the same throughout its long life.

Specimen plants for containers need strong architectural form. Evergreen shrubs that can be clipped into shapes work well in a classical design: large boxwood balls and cubes are especially handsome, while bay looks impressive grown as a standard on a tall stem. Holly also lends itself to this treatment, looking so much more curvaceously chunky and appealing than in its usual loose bush form.

Many exotics thrive happily in tubs. New Zealand flax (*Phormium*) bursts with arching leaf blades in gorgeous shades of bronze and burgundy, some with stripes; *P.* 'Duet' and 'Sundowner' and *P. tenax* 'Purpureum' are among the best varieties. *Yucca filamentosa* 'Bright Edge' and *Y. glauca* form dense crowns of spiny leaves, while the dwarf fan palm (*Chamaerops humilis*) is worth considering for a mild situation.

Bulbs and bedding plants are equally suited to containers. Plant a single variety of spring bulbs, say black *Tulipa* 'Queen of Night' or white lily-of-the-valley (*Convallaria majalis*), in a lead cistern, or try a mass of ivy-leaved pelargonium trailing from a tall Anduze vase for a sensational summer display.

above left *Elaborate terracotta pots and exotic agaves combine in an interesting play of textures and styles. They make a strong structural statement arranged in a row on this brick terrace.*
above right *Weathered zinc introduces a new look to the classical container form. The planter is filled with fragrant, clipped, silvery-grey lavender.*

sculpture and ornament

A piece of sculpture or an elegant ornament is invaluable in a smart courtyard, and nothing can surpass a well-chosen piece for its capacity to captivate, to surprise or even to shock. Examples can be found in a wide variety of styles, so choosing can be difficult, especially since taste is extremely subjective. Reproductions of classical figures are always popular, and if you want to emulate the glories of earlier centuries in your courtyard design, these may be your best option. If you want something a little more unusual, however, why not investigate the possibility of owning the work of a living, breathing sculptor? A piece created as a result of new ideas or a new way of looking at the world, or perhaps even something you have commissioned yourself, will bring untold pleasure and gratification.

Figurative form may seem to be the most natural direction to take in a garden setting, and many people feel that birds, animals and human figures are the most suitable subjects for garden statuary. This view is absolutely valid, although it is advisable to avoid romantic or kitsch cliché, and seek out an interpretation that reveals the intrinsic beast or person. Discover an artist with a true comprehension of character and habit, who will produce a work with strength, warmth and humour, whether the form is animal or human, real or mythical.

Choosing a piece of abstract sculpture is more adventurous, but your appreciation will grow partly through an understanding of the artist's capability to interpret ideas through materials, and partly through the development of your response to form and texture.

The choice of material is dictated by the style of the piece, with wood, stone and marble being used for carvings, while castings are made from bronze, terracotta, resin and cement. Stone is the natural choice for a courtyard; it also provides the perfect medium for calligraphy. Inscribing rock with single letters or words is a subtle form of sculpture that combines elegant lettering with poetry. The inscribed rocks can be fixed to a wall or set in the ground, or perhaps form part of a piece of furniture, such as a bench or table-top. Wood is the other material that naturally belongs in a garden and lends itself to the skills of a sculptor. For example, a simple piece of wood, carved to reveal the grain and colour of a piece of green oak, is a pleasure to touch.

opposite Ancient meets modern in this courtyard garden. Shafts of light and shimmering white flowers are reflected by a steel obelisk, a dazzling reinterpretation of the classical obelisk.
left A stone relic, fallen from a long-gone monastery, lies quietly now in a border.
below This terracotta statue creates a striking focal point in a softly planted courtyard.

feature planting

The built elements of a courtyard provide its basic structure and shape, forming a clean, still backdrop for the planting scheme. Together they should create a harmonious balance, with the hard materials playing a neutral supporting role to the life and energy of the plants. Because the design is concentrated into a restricted area, an ideal opportunity exists to feature rare and unusual species and tender exotics, which benefit from the microclimate in a courtyard.

With many thousands of plants from which to choose, it is useful to identify their individual characters. The personality of a plant is expressed through its habit, shape and leaf form. Spiky individuals are the outgoing party-lovers of the plant world, pushing their way energetically out of the ground and waving about wildly in the breeze. Yuccas, phormiums and aloes make strong statements, especially good for contrast features.

Conversely, small-leaved, mound-forming species are the reclusives, waiting for their quiet beauty to be recognized. Diminutive *Hebe pinguifolia*, with its tiny glaucous leaves, is good for cushioning bed edges, while the feathery cotton lavender (*Santolina chamaecyparissus*) can be set into architectural groups of clipped grey-green spheres.

A clothing of energetic climbers is an essential backdrop in a courtyard. Evergreen *Clematis armandii* will quickly smother a sheltered arbour with its lance-like leaves and produce cascades of delightful white blossom in early spring.

Climbers are the guerillas of the plant world, insinuating their way up walls and through gaps.

Evergreens are the solid citizens, slow-growing, important for the creation of a garden framework, and often best set into groups and clipped to shape. Yew (*Taxus baccata*) and box (*Buxus sempervirens*) are the stars for this treatment, bringing vital structure during the winter and made still more stunning when covered with glittering frost.

Perennials are the showmen, bursting from the earth in spring to create a wealth of forms and textures. The honeybush (*Melianthus major*) can spread its deeply dissected, lime-coloured foliage into huge mounds, 2m (6ft) wide and 1m (3ft) high, while the plume poppy (*Macleaya cordata*) shoots up plumes of cream flowers above a thicket of heart-shaped grey foliage. For sheer style, nothing beats the hosta's dramatic veined foliage; dozens of varieties combine greys, sulphurs and limes, some plain and others with striking margins.

The changing seasons bring a special joy to the gardener. Following the delicate winter tracery of branches, deciduous shrubs and trees erupt with tender foliage in spring, provide shade in summer and produce leaves of gold and bronze with fruits and seeds in autumn. Among the best smaller trees, the birches (*Betula*) offer a combination of delicate foliage to rattle in the breeze and wonderful bark textures.

above *Blue agapanthus rise above softly mounding beds, which gently break the edges of the raised wooden pathway.*
opposite top *Iceberg roses, wisteria standards and creamy violas accent this parterre.*
opposite, below left *Yew (Taxus baccata) can be clipped into any number of shapes.*
opposite, below right *A dramatic planting of tall trees, columnar evergreens and spiky agaves echoes the backdrop of high-rise buildings behind this city courtyard.*

formal courtyard

This sophisticated urban courtyard is a calm and intimate retreat, cleverly conceived to optimize the space within the confines of a period building. Its distinctive contemporary feel demonstrates the owner/designer's ability to reinterpret classical lines and symmetry using modern materials and building techniques.

A garden room admits access to the lower terrace, which is enclosed on one side by a leafy, vine-covered wall and overlooked opposite by the windows of the home office, a welcoming, single-storey, stone building with richly coloured roof tiles. The window frames and wooden door of the outdoor office are painted in a pale duck-egg blue, which tones beautifully with the grey pots and subdued planting throughout the courtyard. Mellow reclaimed

York stone paving slabs have been used for the flooring, but a classical, marble-tile, mosaic floor has been included to create a striking, floor-level focal point in the central area of the paving. Positioned in front of the sliding doors, it can be easily seen from the inside of the house. The soft colours of cream, blue and grey pick up the tones of other materials and finishes in the courtyard.

Raised beds planted with structural evergreens, including pittosporums and *Festuca glauca*, form walls to line the steps to the upper level, which features a quiet, formal pool. High brick walls surround the garden, lined on one side by black bamboo (*Phyllostachys nigra*) and on the return by a bold, mellowed oak pergola. Planting throughout is in architectural blocks following the lines of the hard landscaping, with mop-head olive trees (*Olea europaea*) in aged zinc planters providing the main focal points. The planters have been given a topdressing of gravel as a final finishing touch.

above *The hard landscaping in this courtyard has been executed to a very high standard. The changes of level, using raised beds and flights of steps, occur smoothly, the whole composition being unified with the use throughout of York stone paving.*
left and above left *The formal zinc planters create elegant, understated focal points in this courtyard.*
opposite *The inset of pale-coloured mosaic tiles creates a dramatic visual relief in the York stone paving.*

THE GARDEN PLAN

laying a mosaic tile square

The flooring in a courtyard can be made from a variety of materials. The York stone paving in this elegant courtyard has been embellished on the lower level just outside the house by a square inset of geometric, blue and grey tiles.

1. Plan out your design on paper, allowing for a 5mm (¼in) space between each tile for mortar, and calculate the number of tiles in each colour that will be needed. Note that a deep-tinted mortar will add distinction to the finished design.

2. Plot the area to be tiled by marking out the shape using strings stretched between pegs, taking care to make sure that the corners are at right angles. Allow an extra tolerance along each edge of at least 10cm (4in).

3. Prepare for the foundations by digging down to a depth of about 20cm (8in) to allow for layers of hardcore and sand. Compact the area firmly with a sledgehammer or stout wooden post.

4. Add a layer of hardcore, at least 10cm (4in) deep, and compact this with the sledgehammer.

5. To bind the surface, spread a 5cm (2in) layer of builders' sand over the hardcore. Smooth over the surface with a garden rake and check all the levels.

6. Mark a peg at the finished level for the paving and calculate all the measurements from here. To allow rainwater to drain away, allow for a fall of 1 in 40.

7. Cut the tiles to shape with an angle grinder, taking care to follow safety regulations. Arrange them in the desired pattern to be sure of the design.

8. Starting in the centre of the floor and working in an area of about 30cm (12in) at a time, dab mortar on the sand where each tile will lie, then position the tiles, adding a small dab to their edges. Tap down each tile gently. Use a spirit level to check levels in both directions.

9. Continue with each section until the design is finished. A long straight edge will help you to control the levels as the work progresses.

10. When all the tiles are laid, work mortar into all the 5mm (¼in) gaps that were left between the tiles. This gives a neat effect and prevents rainwater running into the cracks. Brush away any surplus mortar before it hardens.

Reclaimed York stone flags

Vitis vinifera **'Purpurea'**

plant list

1 *Vitis vinifera*
2 *Pittosporum tobira* 'Wheeler's Dwarf'
3 *Olea europaea*
4 *Festuca glauca* 'Blausilber'
5 *Phyllostachys nigra*

left *The raised bed is planted with Pittosporum tobira 'Wheeler's Dwarf', a small-leaved form of the species, which is grown as a foliage plant. Its compact, bushy habit makes an excellent foil to the tall, narrow planting space.*

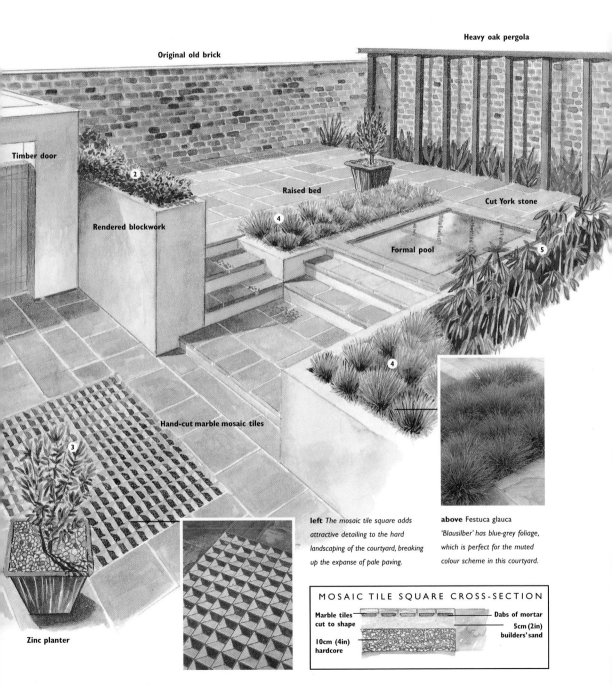

Heavy oak pergola

Original old brick

Timber door

Rendered blockwork

2

Raised bed

4

Cut York stone

Formal pool

5

Hand-cut marble mosaic tiles

4

3

Zinc planter

left *The mosaic tile square adds attractive detailing to the hard landscaping of the courtyard, breaking up the expanse of pale paving.*

above *Festuca glauca 'Blausilber' has blue-grey foliage, which is perfect for the muted colour scheme in this courtyard.*

MOSAIC TILE SQUARE CROSS-SECTION

Marble tiles cut to shape

Dabs of mortar

10cm (4in) hardcore

5cm (2in) builders' sand

How pleasant on a balmy evening to sit with friends around a candlelit supper table, knowing that you can curl up later in a gently swaying swing seat under the stars, with some soothing music playing in the background. Eating outside, surrounded by the fragrance of night-scented flowers, is a marvellously simple yet rewarding way to enjoy your garden, and a courtyard provides the perfect setting. The theatrical potential of a courtyard also comes to the fore after sundown, when lighting can create an air of mystery and romance for relaxing and entertaining.

PLACES TO

entertain

A courtyard or terrace suits outdoor entertaining perfectly, with enclosing walls and perhaps a shaded arbour providing just the right degree of privacy for a summer lunch or full-scale party. The courtyard garden is a real-life stage set that can be dressed for the evening with candles and flowers, fabrics and cushions. Trees become shadowy forms and white flowers gleam eerily, while water develops a velvety depth and sounds take on a new vibrancy.

You might like to create a special theme for a party or event, whether this is formal, exotic or romantic. Let your guests discover the moonlit terrace studded with tiny uplighters around its edges. When the mood quietens, play soft music through a subtle sound system of speakers set in the ground, and warm the air with portable gas-space heaters if the temperature drops too low.

A low seating area under a tented canopy, lit by candles and suffused with drifting incense, will certainly bring out a spirit of adventure in your diners, inspiring thoughts of deserts, Moguls and daring deeds. Sit your guests on huge cushions among pots of heady jasmine, and theme the food to suit the evening, with bowls of fragrant rice and spiced vegetables.

If by night the courtyard is all soft lighting and shadows, by day it is brought into focus with clear light and solid form. Colour and texture are now the key, with bright climbers adorning walls and flowers spilling from containers. Late breakfasts may be taken in style, with nothing more than birdsong and trickling water to break the silence. By lunchtime, tents and canopies can shade guests from the midday sun, while they bask in the scent of roses and honeysuckle.

opposite *An olive tree in a plain zinc planter complements the metal steps and door.* **below** *The pure lines of this modern roof terrace demand an understated treatment. A canopy provides privacy and protection from sunlight. The sitting area is framed between a curved bench, a shallow rill of water and the minimal planting.* **previous page** *The generous wooden table and chairs are perfect for relaxed entertaining.*

furniture

The central focus for an entertainer's courtyard is the furniture. A generous-sized dining table is a must for social gatherings, and the accompanying chairs should be both comfortable during long relaxed meals and light enough to move around for parties. Some comfortable loungers are always welcome where space permits, and perhaps a bench or two for quiet corners.

The decision about furniture style is subjective and depends on taste and lifestyle, but the matter of construction material, be it wood, metal or synthetics, needs a pragmatic approach. Outdoor equipment has to cope with the toll of sun, rain and fluctuating temperatures, so it must be built to an exacting specification to tolerate the inevitable stresses of expansion, contraction and corrosion. All garden furniture benefits from winter protection. Either move it into a garage or shed, or perhaps into a conservatory (sun room), or cover it *in situ* with waterproof covers.

Hardwood is the premier product out of doors; it is tough and durable, and blends naturally among plants, maturing gently to a silvery patina. A good-quality product can give a lifetime's service, easily justifying a higher cost price. A recent trend to move away from the bulkier traditional designs for which wood is known has resulted in the welcome appearance of pared-down, lighter-weight forms. Many of these are foldable for storage, making them ideal for a courtyard garden.

Admired for its smooth grain and durability, teak was always the wood of choice. It is becoming scarcer now, due to dubious forestry practices over the past few decades, so alternatives like iroko are now appearing, along with luxury hardwoods such as oak. You can ask your retailer for certification that the furniture has been made from managed, plantation-grown wood. Alternatively, seek out eco-friendly pieces created from reclaimed wood. Whichever hardwood you use, give it a good coat of teak oil at the start and end of the summer in order to feed and protect it.

Softwood, from quick-growing coniferous trees, is relatively inexpensive and also widely available. Though less durable than hardwood, a painted finish or, even better, a maintenance-free, tinted wood stain will help to keep softwood furniture looking sharp and fresh. Incorporate it into your decorating scheme, matching it to planters and screens, and accenting it with colourful cushions and parasols.

opposite *A table and chairs are an essential part of a courtyard designed for entertaining, but these beautiful hand-built pieces also provide a sculptural focal point within the design of a slate terrace.*
left *You know a chair is comfortable when the cat chooses to sit on it.*
below *Huge floor cushions for lounging are a relaxing and pleasantly informal alternative to chairs. Moveable slatted screens also provide privacy and seclusion, while admitting light and the heady scent of gardenias.*

Iron and steel naturally oxidize in open air, so only factory-galvanized products have a chance of remaining maintenance-free outdoors. Some of the most useful are lightweight, romantically styled, terrace dining sets, with chairs and table-tops of fine mesh. A decorative bench of forged steel makes an elegant place to rest, but this material's weight and total rigidity make it uncomfortable for dining chairs at the table. Wirework is a much better option here, being comfortable, light and flexible. The pretty reproductions of classic nineteenth-century designs can be brought right up to date by painting them in deep Chinese lacquer tones.

Synthetic materials have moved on tremendously in the past decade, contributing to some of the most exciting contemporary furniture designs. Shell-shaped seats made from textile or plastic and combined with aluminium frames are both lightweight and stackable. They also require little or no maintenance. Ideal for small spaces with limited storage, many pieces can also be used for indoor dining.

A parasol is essential in daytime to shade guests from the sun, while at night it gives a sense of containment to the setting. Ensure that it is both generously proportioned and adjustable to accommodate the varying angles of the sun as it moves through the sky. Colours of cream, ivory and sand give shade without the oppressive heaviness of dark tones, but to keep these looking good you should choose a stain-resistant finish. This is especially important in the city, where rain brings down airborne grime. Parasols can be astonishingly heavy, so a mechanical cranking system is advisable; electrically operated systems do exist, but the machinery is rather too bulky to be discreet. Lighting can be built into the parasol, either with a central spot or, more prettily, by clear plastic tubes filled with tiny lamps fixed along the spokes.

A canopy strung between walls makes an inexpensive and effective way to shade a terrace, creating a romantic atmosphere with the minimum of fuss. Make it from filmy gauze, robust canvas or striped ticking, depending upon the effect desired, and string it between opposite or right-angled walls with heavy-duty bolts. Beneath the canopy, a low table framed by cushion-strewn benches can create an understated dining arrangement. As an alternative to fabric, sea-grass cushions and mattresses have a refreshingly new feel for relaxed outdoor living. A vibrantly striped hammock is welcome, too, for hot, dreamy afternoons and gentle relaxation.

right *Lightweight aluminium and nylon sun loungers are perfect for relaxing, and can be easily folded away.*

opposite top *Natural hardwood can be left outside all year round. In summer, a parasol is crucial for dining.*

opposite, below left *Stacking chairs are useful in a small space. This plastic and aluminium chair is matched perfectly by the metal table.*

opposite, below right *A glass-topped table and nylon slatted chairs give an ethereal look to this tiny, tropical terrace.*

lighting

You can invariably produce a magical effect with lighting, and an imaginatively designed scheme can transform a courtyard into a theatre of contrasting shapes and moods. It extends the physical use of the courtyard from daytime to the evening, while also creating a romantic night-time landscape to view from the house.

Lighting should work in subtle combinations to achieve its aims. Never harsh or overly bright, it should be used to highlight interesting features while gently suffusing the background scene. When cleverly positioned, it can completely alter the perception of scale and space.

There are many components with which to develop low-voltage systems. Uplighting is the most versatile and can be used in varying densities and styles, depending upon the effect required. At its simplest, it works well as a broad beam under a tree to emphasize the silhouette or throw a fascinating pattern of shadows from the branches, while for sharper focus, angled spotlights can highlight a piece of sculpture or a feature such as a gazebo. Used in a group, soft floodlights set low in a shrub border will reveal just its subtle contours.

Spotlights are also great for achieving special effects under water, bringing a translucent luminosity to a pool or highlighting the movements of a fountain or cascade. They can throw dynamic shadows through a latticed obelisk or give a surreal, floating feeling to a glass sculpture. Individual spots are practical and look

above *Oil-burning torches lend a real sense of drama and a theatrical glamour to parties once the sun has gone down.*

below left *Interior backlighting provides a distinctive atmosphere at this stylish home, the slatted window treatments and sculptural garden plants adding shadows and glinting reflections around the deep black pool.*
right *Interior and underwater spotlighting connects the pool with the house at night, here creating a towering, galleried vista of spiky architectural planting and objets d'art.*

dramatic when set in rows into paving to define a pool edge or outline a path and steps. Mini-spots set into wooden or metal posts are easy to install and useful for entrances or along pathways.

A reverse effect can be achieved using gentle downwash lights to reveal texture on walls and surfaces. Used in conjunction with interior lighting through large picture windows, these lights throw the focus back to the house, leaving the terrace backlit to very dramatic effect.

For a natural approach, nothing is more soothing and flattering than candlelight, and nothing is easier to place. For table centres, flickering, coloured tea-lights create a romantic ambience, while oversized glass hurricane lamps make a handsome style statement. For background effect, set tea-lights by the dozen along walls and steps in glass jars to prevent them being blown out in the breeze. At the other end of the scale, huge column candles, 1.5m (5ft) high, make truly dramatic statements, while metal oil lamps on tall stems introduce a kind of medieval splendour and can be easily pushed into the ground to accentuate entrances and paths for parties.

Also brilliant for stage work, fairy lights are making a sophisticated renaissance. Now appearing twined into fragile drapes, they make a delicate backdrop when fixed to the framework of a dining canopy or screen; use them in winter, too, for a pretty icicle effect along a veranda.

A practical note here is important: electricity out of doors is too dangerous for the amateur to install, so get a qualified electrician to do the job for you. A lighting designer will achieve the best visual effects and should be called in at an early stage in your courtyard design so that the cable can be laid during the construction. However, there are solar-powered lights now available that do not need electrical cables.

above left *Pretty glass tea-lights are ideal for the courtyard because they protect the flames from the wind.*
left *Brilliant spotlights transform a smooth slate fountain into a boiling cauldron of light and fire at night.*
right *Lighting from below can result in subtle and unexpected effects. At this creative city conversion, uplit palms tower over a surreal illuminated glass bridge, casting immense shadows on the opposite wall.*

sound

above left *Bamboo wind chimes lend a pleasantly authentic atmosphere to a Japanese-style courtyard.*

above centre *A gentle stream of water creates a trickling sound as it falls down through a series of ceramic beakers that form part of a wall-mounted set piece.*

above right *A narrow waist-high rill splashes noisily into a quirky arrangement of copper cans.*

The effect of lighting in a courtyard is obvious, but sound invisibly contributes to the ambience of the space in a more subtle way. Sound creeps up on a tranquil listener. The gentlest breeze is enough to disturb the leaves of some plants, causing grasses to swish and poplars to rattle, while birdsong at dawn is a truly uplifting sound, especially appreciated by urbanites.

Natural sounds are a real bonus in any town courtyard and can be encouraged by the choice of planting. Buzzing insects, for example, will flock around summer flowers, with lavender (*Lavandula*) and thyme (*Thymus*) being firm favourites with bees. Eucalyptus and bamboos both respond co-operatively to wind, creating an audiovisual kaleidoscope of moving foliage.

The ever-popular wind chime can also be used to bring sound into a courtyard, capturing the breeze to produce a variety of soothing sounds, ranging from tinkling bells to flat Eastern tones. A metal chime will also gleam attractively, either hung in a tree or suspended from a pergola.

Water features will bring a host of interesting sounds to the courtyard garden, and will be appreciated by visiting wildlife. Water, which sparkles in sunlight and reflects shadows and shapes, can be organized in a diversity of forms from a gurgling fall to a still, shallow pool in which birds can splash and bathe.

The different possibilities for water features are endless, but if the aim is to provide a romantic effect, a pool with a sprinkling fountain makes an eye-catching focal point, especially when planted with white water lilies such as *Nymphaea* 'Odorata Alba' to glow in evening floodlight. By contrast, for sheer drama, create a gushing cascade down a vertical surface; reflective materials like polished granite, bright steel or backlit glass are effective, either freestanding or set against a boundary wall.

When selecting sound effects for the courtyard, consider your proximity to your neighbours, who will probably not want to have their peace shattered by your sounds. Sound can bounce from hard surfaces in an enclosed area, where the effect of a vigorous cascade or fast-moving water gurgling over stones can be overwhelming, while constant trickling may become irritating over time. Force and sound can be manipulated by adjusting the pump, and it is a case of experimenting until the desired effect is achieved.

Strictly for occasional and controlled use, a sound system with tiny speakers partly buried in the ground or set in paving can introduce soft music themed to the food and decoration. Try introducing atmospheric tapes of natural sounds, like tropical birds at an evening watering hole, dawn in an Australian rainforest or waves breaking on a beach.

above left *Surely the most decadent cocktail bar. Champagne bottles cool under a steady stream of flowing water, which then plunges loudly in a broad smooth curtain into the iris-lined canal below.*
above right *A lively cascade gushes noisily, but invitingly, into a deep, pale aquamarine plunge pool.*

plants for scent and colour

A warm evening releases the perfumes of flowers, bringing a sense of romance to your courtyard. Musky tobacco plants (*Nicotiana*), stocks (*Matthiola incana*) and night-scented stocks (*M. bicornis*) are terrific for scented seasonal bedding, while shrubby evergreen Japanese mock orange (*Pittosporum tobira*) and Mexican orange blossom (*Choisya ternata*) reward year after year with their sweet citrus-like scent. Ravishing, but poisonous, datura (*Brugmansia*) waits until dusk before releasing its fragrance to attract night-time pollinators to its huge, dangling bells, while equally tender gardenias and stephanotis will enrich a table setting with their evocative perfume.

Lilies (*Lilium*) have a luxurious glamour to match their perfume, while, for sheer elegance, agapanthus is an absolute diva, with starburst blooms carried on tall stems. Cheerful rock roses, *Cistus* × *aguilari* and *C. ladanifer*, and lavish *Paeonia suffruticosa* 'Rock's Variety', a tree peony with a red-stained centre, are brightly coloured, while white-flowered *Convolvulus cneorum* also has soft, silver foliage. For large scale and texture, silvery sea holly (*Eryngium maritimum*) and deeply incised cardoon (*Cynara cardunculus*) are hard to beat. The dahlia, with its showy blooms, is wonderful for late-summer drama. The styles and cultivars are too numerous to mention here, but be prepared to experiment with mixes, clashing shocking pinks with orange and dark crimsons with brilliant yellow.

Pots bursting with vivacious bedding plants play a supporting role on the terrace. Endless combinations can be made of blue and pink petunias, scarlet and orange busy Lizzies (*Impatiens*), orange marigolds (*Tagetes*) and nasturtiums (*Tropaeolum majus*) or, more grandly, pelargoniums in bold pinks and deep reds.

Climbers add an extra dimension, enclosing arbours and pergolas with scent. Jasmine (*Jasminum polyanthum*) and evergreen star jasmine (*Trachelospermum jasminoides*) have an Eastern-style perfume, while roses like 'Albéric Barbier' and 'Madame Alfred Carrière' have an old-fashioned fragrance. As a bonus, all these flowers are white (or have white forms), so they will glow at night in reflected light. For daytime impact, colourful climbers are ideal. A passion flower such as purple *Passiflora* 'Amethyst' is a must for a sheltered spot, while blue *P. caerulea* will produce showy orange fruits on a sunny wall. It is easy to include a good selection of clematis, as these can be grown on tripods for spot features as well as on wall trellis. Unbeatable scramblers for hot climates are the purple, orange and red bougainvilleas, offset by soft, powdery blue plumbago.

opposite *Brilliant colours are immediately cheering. Pots of herbs, steps lined with vivacious bougainvillea, and a balcony dripping with fragrant jasmine create a seductive seating area.*
left *A verdigris cauldron planted with fragrant pinks (Dianthus) provides pretty decoration in the courtyard.*
below *This brightly painted, low wall separates parts of the courtyard and provides a convenient seating ledge. Colourful pots of pansies provide a link with the border of plants beyond.*

moroccan nights

A vibrant Moroccan theme reverberates through this sensual courtyard, lushly planted with climbers, architectural palms and colourful, perfumed flowers. Castellated parapets and Arabian-style keyhole doorways define the high, enclosing walls. Rendered and painted a soft pink to match the pale terracotta paving, both are relieved by the blue-and-gold mosaic-tiled surface cladding and floor insets.

An intimate, plant-filled alcove, enclosed by tall, tile-clad columns, provides a cosy seating area set with a comfortable bench, while a quiet viewing niche contains a metal table and chairs for relaxed dining and entertaining. The table is set with opulent blue and gold bowls and plates. The bench, invitingly covered with colourful rugs and velvet cushions, is perfect for passing a few idle hours or for relaxing with friends after an *al fresco* candlelit meal. The alcove also contains a marble bowl

placed on a tile plinth in order to provide a gentle splash of water. The reservoir holding the bowl is shallow and tiled with ceramic glazed tiles.

Vertical interest is further provided by changes of level, with blue and yellow tiled steps leading down to a lower terrace. The main point-of-interest of this lower area is a dramatic, long, formal pool. This is dominated by a tall, wrought-iron minaret, based on the minaret at the Hassen II mosque. Beneath this, on a submerged plinth, sits an elegant amphora jar planted with an exotic *Agave americana* 'Variegata'. The still water of the pool makes it ideal for growing the elegant white waterlily *Nymphaea* 'Gladstoneana'. The pool is traversed by two square stepping stones, which bring the viewer closer still to the tranquil water.

above *The castellated walls surrounding the courtyard give a real sense of an ancient Moroccan citadel.*
above left *Such a dramatic setting calls for an equally exotic feast. This courtyard lends itself to a themed party.*
left *Arabian-style keyhole doorways add interest to the high walls, the neutral colour of which provides a good foil for the colourful planting.*
opposite *The table and chairs on the upper terrace of the courtyard create the perfect setting for an evening meal.*

THE GARDEN PLAN

building a flight of steps

Changes of level add interest to a small garden, and a shallow flight of steps can be created fairly easily without the help of a professional builder. Plan the steps carefully and choose materials that will integrate naturally with their surroundings.

1. Plan out the area, measuring the overall height from top to bottom and the available width, which should be at least 1.5m (5ft). Shallow steps work best in the garden, so the height of each riser should be 10–15cm (4–6in) and the depth (front to back) of each tread should be 30–45cm (12–18in). Draw a cross-section on squared paper to calculate the number of steps needed, adjusting the depth and gradient to fit the space.

2. Excavate and lay a concrete foundation under the area of the steps, extending it slightly in front of the first riser. When

the concrete is dry, lay a course of bricks bedded in mortar to form the first riser.
3. Infill behind it with hardcore and consolidate it firmly by tamping it down with a wooden post.
4. Lay a mortar bed to the depth of the tread over the bricks and hardcore. Set in the stone tread so that it projects over the riser by about 2.5cm (1in). Check the level of the slabs with a spirit level to make sure that there is a slight run-off for rainwater.
5. Spread a layer of mortar along the back of the tread and lay a course of bricks over the stone slab to form the second riser.
6. Infill once more with hardcore, then consolidate and lay the stone tread as before.
7. Continue laying each step, checking the levels at each step to ensure a slight slope for water run-off. The top tread should finish level with the upper ground surface.
8. Blue and yellow, glazed ceramic tiles can be mortared to the riser of each step.

above *The tiled flights of stairs lead to a colourful terrace with a table and chairs for outdoor dining.*

***Agave americana* 'Variegata'**

plant list
 1 *Chamaerops humilis*
 2 *Phormium tenax* 'Purpureum Group'
 3 *Achillea filipendulina* 'Cloth of Gold'
 4 *Rosa* 'Irish Eyes'
 5 *Griselinia littoralis*
 6 *Helenium* 'Wyndley'
 7 *Canna* 'Roitelet'
 8 *Rosmarinus officinalis*
 9 *Convolvulus cneorum*
 10 *Phygelius* 'African Queen'
 11 *Nymphaea* 'Gladstoneana'
 12 *Sisyrinchium californicum*

 13 *Agave americana*
 14 *Heuchera micrantha* var. *diversifolia* 'Palace Purple'
 15 *Tagetes* Gem Series
 16 *Artemisia* 'Boughton Silver'
 17 *Hakonechloa macra* 'Aureola'
 18 *Agave americana* 'Variegata'
 19 *Fatsia japonica*
 20 *Rosa* 'Snowball'
 21 *Arundo donax*
 22 *Onopordum acanthium*
 23 *Cercis canadensis* 'Forest Pansy'
 24 *Cytisus battandieri*

Wrought-iron minaret

Rendered block wall

Moroccan-style pillars

23

22

21

18

Amphora jar

6

20

19

above *Based on the minaret of the Hassen II mosque, this wrought-iron sculpture gives height to the garden and casts an elegant reflection in the pool.*

12   13

15   17

14   16

Steps

Long pool

11

Neutral paving, inset with blue-glazed ceramic tiles

left *The sumptuous colours and textures of the planting in this courtyard, such as yellow achilleas, orange cannas and golden heleniums, are perfect for its exotic theme. The bold stems of Kniphofia 'Royal Standard' look striking against the walls.*

FLIGHT OF STEPS CROSS-SECTION

Stone tread

Brick riser

Mortar

Compacted hardcore

Concrete foundation slab

Some people are lucky enough to live in the country where a beautiful rural courtyard is easy to achieve. Others, while dreaming of life in the country, realise how much an urban existence offers in the way of convenience for work, shopping, entertainment and culture. Rather than giving up thoughts of country life altogether, why not bring some of the countryside into your urban existence by way of a courtyard garden? A country-style courtyard is the perfect setting for mixing in some edible produce with the flowers, and few things can be more satisfying than preparing a meal from home-grown vegetables, herbs and fruit.

COUNTRY

eden

Creating a flower-filled, country-style atmosphere calls for a natural approach to the design of the courtyard as well as the choice of plants. The typical country courtyard, whether it is actually in the country or in an urban environment, has a relaxed, informal approach, with crunchy gravel paths, an abundance of tumbling plants and climber-clad decorative structures such as arches and arbours. Details such as old water butts, rusty metal furniture and weathered terracotta pots are another strong feature of the country courtyard.

There is also the welcome opportunity to grow a wealth of traditional cottage-garden plants, including hollyhocks, lupins, delphiniums, columbines and daisies as well as the ubiquitous scented roses. The planting can seem artless and unplanned, a riot of colours, textures and scents.

The country-style courtyard is the perfect setting for growing some vegetables, fruit or herbs. It is surprising how well a framework of decorative shrubs and perennial flowers will combine with home-grown crops. Climbing roses, honeysuckle and golden hop can all be trained on walls, fences and arbours, while a main feature can be made of a plum or cherry tree in a handsome tub. A sunny bed could be given a Mediterranean flavour, combining globe artichokes with verbascum for height, underplanted with a scented collection of lavenders and thyme, sage and rue.

If space is at a premium, you will be amazed how much edible produce can be grown in a raised bed or collection of purpose-built containers. You can easily grow a few salad ingredients in a collection of pots, herbs in a window box and even a few potatoes in a barrel, in perfect harmony with the flowers.

opposite *In this inviting country retreat, a metal heron watches over a fish pool, while weather-beaten chairs are positioned in a corner.*
below *The entrance at the back of a house is an ideal location for a mass display. This collection of old terracotta pots is arranged to achieve a stylishly "casual" result.*
previous page *Even a country-style courtyard in the city has room for an old potting shed.*

country courtyards

Whether you live in the country and want to create a small, courtyard-style, country garden, or whether you are seeking to bring a country feel to an urban courtyard, try to aim for a relaxed, informal atmosphere. The traditional cottage garden is one where the plants seem to proliferate everywhere, with an abundance of scented climbers, containers with brightly coloured flowers and informal ornaments.

A country courtyard is an idyllic retreat in which to recharge your batteries. If you favour just such a romantic wilderness where you can escape from urban life, then plant sweeping swathes of perennials for a sense of drama as well as to provide interesting textures and a plethora of different flower forms. Introduce colourful annual bedding in pots and blooming climbers to scramble up walls and trellis. Insects and birds will flock to these pollen-laden blooms, energy-giving seed-heads and bowls of life-enhancing water, rewarding you with their songs and vitality.

A **country** courtyard brings with it the gentle hum of insects and the fragrance of summer flowers.

Free form in planning is the key, using curved beds that allow a change of shape every time you find it impossible to live without several more choice finds at a plant sale. Eventually you may find that the growing beds and borders have encroached on to all the lawned areas of the courtyard.

above *Charming animal sculptures like this intrepid wire-mesh chicken bring a sense of fun to a courtyard.*
opposite *An overflowing planting of perennials and climbers is perfect in this informal terrace, while old cobble paving and a comfortable basket chair add a further touch of country chic.*

Create three-dimensional pictures with tall-growing verbascums, sunflowers (*Helianthus*) and hollyhocks (*Alcea*), adding twiggy wigwams for climbing nasturtiums (*Tropaeolum majus*) and sweet peas (*Lathyrus*). Use colour like a paint palette to create hot spots of orange, red and yellow with day lilies (*Hemerocallis*), red hot pokers (*Kniphofia*), cannas and rudbeckias, clashing with the bright pinks and purples of dahlias, penstemons and cranesbills (*Geranium*).

There can never be too much blue in a garden, and using these tones in drifts toward the boundaries will lend an illusion of distance in a courtyard. Agapanthus, salvias and monkshoods (*Aconitum*) offer tall-standing spikes, while the combination of forms and texture is completed with ground-hugging campanulas, sweet violets (*Viola odorata*) and colourful pansies (*Viola* x *wittrockiana*). The cooling effect of blue teams well with white flowers to sparkle by day and gleam at night, bringing a sense of peace at the end of a stressful day. Standing high above a blue mist, stately windflowers (*Anemone*)

appear late in the season after columns of delphiniums in summer, while the scents of tobacco plants (*Nicotiana*), stocks (*Matthiola*) and lilies (*Lilium*) pervade a warm evening.

Make some space where you can immerse yourself in your haven of tranquillity. Place a simple table with a couple of chairs to enjoy a leisurely breakfast. Make a seating arbour where the perfumes can be enjoyed at sunset, and train sweet-smelling honeysuckle (*Lonicera*) or jasmine (*Jasminum*) to add to the sensual effect.

above *Second-hand shops are a rich source of country antiques such as this old zinc washing tub and sink. Planted with flowering herbs and brilliant iris, they bring just the right tone of "urban country".*

opposite *Vegetables and flowers mix surprisingly well in this burgeoning courtyard. Roses scramble among cabbages and sweet violets nestle below tall cane tripods that are ready to support climbing beans.*

potagers and parterres

Vegetables lend themselves to a formal garden design, where they can be organized into easily maintained rows and plots. This serves to emphasize their individual characteristics of form and colour. With this in mind, the ever style-conscious French conceived the idea of the potager, which is a small, walled garden devoted to growing vegetables and laid out in a formal grid. A courtyard version of the potager involves adapting the notion of a parterre – a formally arranged flower garden – for the growth of one particular type of fruit or vegetable. An attractive and delicious option would be to

devote a parterre to a summer-salad garden, including colourful leaves and fruits, accompanied by edible and scented flowers such as nasturtiums (*Tropaeolum majus*) and sweet violets (*Viola odorata*), along with aromatic herbs.

Select a central space in the courtyard that is open and sunny, and mark it out into regular compartments of triangles or rectangles. These should radiate from a central hub, allowing for access paths between them. If there is adequate space, edge the beds with a low evergreen hedge to maintain a strong visual structure throughout the year; otherwise, finish them with a border of woven willow hurdle, and plant with seasonal bedding in the winter months. The conventional choice for a low hedge is deep green box (*Buxus sempervirens* 'Suffruticosa'), though miniature white lavenders, such as *Lavandula angustifolia* 'Nana Alba', or creamy cotton lavender (*Santolina chamaecyparissus* 'Lemon Queen') would bring a further aromatic dimension to the design.

For visual impact, dedicate each compartment of the parterre to a single type of plant. Salad leaves offer a wide variety of shapes and textures that can be combined to make a colourful and productive display. These range from the tightly crisp green varieties like 'Little Gem' and 'Tom Thumb', through to the softly curvaceous picking leaf forms, including 'Salad Bowl', dramatic purple 'Lollo Rosso' and red-tinged 'Sangria'.

Fresh herbs are a vital constituent in the potager. If space is limited, use them as edgings rather than devoting a whole compartment to them. Softly mounding 'Moss Curled' parsley and clump-forming, grass-like chives (*Allium schoenoprasum*) have a suitable habit. If you do have sufficient space, then the forms of fragrant and colourful thymes (*Thymus*) that are available, including low creepers and bushes of various sizes, can be successfully combined in a single compartment.

Include a section for edible flowers, too. These can make an unusual and fragrant addition to drinks, salads, rice dishes and puddings. Nasturtiums are versatile, having peppery edible leaves and flowers

in brilliant yellow, orange and red. 'Empress of India' is particularly rich, with dark, almost violet, leaves and crimson, scented flowers; 'Peach Melba' would provide an excellent contrast in colour. Orange and golden yellow pot marigolds (*Calendula*) liven up a salad when the petals are sprinkled on top. The charming mauve blooms of the sweet violet and pretty clove pinks (*Dianthus caryophyllus*) can both be used in salads and puddings, and rosemary's tiny blue flowers are good for freezing in ice cubes for summer drinks.

Finally, no summer dining table would be complete without a plate of luscious red tomatoes. Grown in a selection of old terracotta pots, the tomatoes could create a delicious, but decorative, centrepiece at the central hub of the parterre. Combine different heritage varieties to make an unusual and flavoursome collection of yellow, red and green.

above *Full use is made of the architecture in this country courtyard. The walls are clothed with climbing hydrangea, while golden hops trail from a pergola. Gravel paths are lined with stone setts and a cast-iron fountain plays gently as a centrepiece.*

opposite *In this lovely mixed parterre, the triangular beds are edged with box. Vegetables, such as red and green salad leaves, are used to form a geometric pattern beside yellow feverfew and orange marigolds.*

below *Informal mosaic adds charming detail to this bed of parsley and lettuce.*

vertical produce

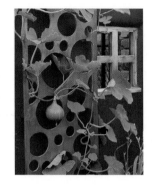

Exploiting the vertical dimension means that you can utilize every bit of space in a small courtyard. Boundaries offer instant backdrops for training fruit trees and climbers, while arbours and arches, as well as temporary features such as tripods, offer a multitude of edible and decorative possibilities. A small arbour trained with fruits like grapes or with more unconventional soft fruits, such as a tayberry or thornless blackberry, would make a good central feature.

The warmth and shelter provided by sun-baked brick walls enable tender fruits such as peaches and apricots to flourish, while cooler, less sunny aspects are more suitable for apples and pears. The practice of espalier training, whereby branches are drawn out on a horizontal plane, is both ornamental and practical, ensuring the maximum amount of light and warmth is available to ripen the fruit. Tall-growing vine tomatoes also benefit from such support and shelter; 'Gardener's Delight', with its huge trusses of cherry tomatoes, striped 'Tigerella' and 'Yellow Perfection' are all well-flavoured and thrive on a sunny wall.

Stone fruits, including plums and cherries, and heat-seeking figs respond well to being trained into fan shapes on a sunny wall, where they will ripen early with heavy crops. Wooden fences do not retain as much warmth as walls, though they can be painted black to increase their heat absorbency. They can be wired or clad in trellis to provide a grid of tying positions for climbing squashes such as 'Pumpkin' and 'Delicata'.

The decorative qualities of climbing vegetables should not be underestimated, and the flowers of runner beans immediately suggest a country garden; try pink 'Sunset', white 'Desiree' and 'Painted Lady', splashed with red and white. For total glamour, the unstoppable hyacinth bean (*Lablab niger*) is a true prima donna: the cerise flowers are followed by enormously long, gleaming, purple pods. Beans need to twine around tall poles or strings, which can be organized into tripod shapes set among low-growing beds to extend the available space. You can make your own each year from bamboo canes and hazel stems, or buy purpose-made metal versions that will last indefinitely.

Tripods and obelisks have the advantage of providing instant architectural effect and can support annual flowers when not required for beans or squashes. Canary creeper (*Tropaeolum peregrinum*), morning glory (*Ipomoea*) and black-eyed Susan (*Thunbergia alata*) all have an informal cottage-garden look, giving their all for one season.

raised beds and containers

Two main difficulties can be experienced when creating a vegetable plot in an enclosed space: insufficient sunlight and poor soil. Creating raised beds within retaining walls should, however, help to remedy both problems at once by increasing the soil depth and bringing plants closer to the sun. Retaining brick walls are smart, but walls built of breeze (cinder) blocks can be given a range of treatments to change their utilitarian look. They can be rendered and painted, faced with ceramic tiles or an exotic mosaic, or clad with wattle for a rustic effect. Heavy timbers and railway sleepers (ties) are easier alternatives, being strong and needing no foundations.

Good drainage is vital, so build on open ground that has been cleared of perennial weeds and dug over to break up the soil. When excavating the foundations for brick and block walls, remove an extra 15cm (6in) of soil and add a layer of rubble (from ground clearing) or gravel to help with drainage before starting to lay the bricks. In addition, create drainage holes at the base of the walls.

On a roof terrace or any area of paving, large containers can take the place of raised beds. Constructed on site from marine ply, they can be freestanding or built to fit against walls, with drainage and irrigation systems incorporated at the design stage. A painted or stained finish is an option; alternatively, they can be clad in galvanized or stainless steel sheeting. Containers can be made to any depth or volume, but weight is an essential consideration when working on roof terraces, so check with a structural engineer that your roof is adequately reinforced before making your plans.

The raised beds or containers must be filled with good-quality topsoil, which can be delivered in bulk by a landscape supplier. Once the topsoil has been delivered, you need to incorporate a good quantity of bulky, well-rotted organic manure.

All kinds of herbs and vegetables can be grown in raised beds and containers. To make the most of the space, plan out your planting scheme to take account of shape, habit and picking time. Aubergines (eggplants) and bell peppers make reasonably compact bushes, while cutting herbs such as coriander (cilantro), rocket (arugula) and parsley make a decorative border. Keep the sunny spots for tomatoes, and give them a good-sized space with basil beneath them. Sun-loving Mediterranean herbs such as rosemary, thyme and sage can tolerate a lot of exposure, whereas lettuces need shade and shelter to thrive.

opposite *A formal style has been adopted with great success in this city terrace. A brick-edged raised bed allows the plants to receive the maximum amount of sunlight. The massed effect of rows of mop-head bay trees, box spheres, thyme and lavender suggests the grandeur of an eighteenth-century parterre.*
left *These pretty violas make a decorative feature on the flight of steps down to a courtyard.*
below *Purpose-made galvanized containers can be filled with grow-bag potting mix to cultivate a wide selection of vegetables, herbs and salads.*

CASE STUDY

edible bounty

This lush potager is framed by a handsome evergreen hedge, which gives both definition to the space as well as a background to the planting. Practicality is as important as good looks in a courtyard garden that is largely devoted to growing edible produce, in this case mainly vegetables and pungent herbs such as rosemary and thyme.

The area is divided up into manageably proportioned beds that are contained within sturdy wooden retaining walls. This gives an agreeably rustic appearance to the overall design. The pathways between the beds are wide enough for the passage of wheelbarrows, making tending the plots that much easier. In fact, it is possible to reach every part of each bed from the path, so avoiding walking directly on the soil. The paths are covered with gravel chippings, which are easy to keep clean with a garden rake. The whole effect is one of neat efficiency.

The vertical dimension is especially important when the majority of the planting is low growing. Here, a bold wooden archway, which is suitable for training woody climbing subjects such as vines (*Vitis*) or scented roses, has been erected at the entrance to the courtyard area. Stylish climbing frames constructed of wooden T-sections and suspended chains also give added height to the beds and could be used to support pole beans or squashes.

above and opposite *The bed is retained with solid wooden railway sleepers (ties). This allows for easy access to the bed for tending the produce.*
above left *Not only do pot marigolds (*Calendula officinalis*) add a splash of colour to the vegetable bed, but they also ward off unwelcome pests and diseases.*
left *The beds are arranged in a circle, rather like the spokes of a wheel, and are filled with vegetables and herbs as well as flowers such as French lavender (*Lavandula stoechas*).*

THE GARDEN PLAN

building a low raised bed

Both decorative and practical, raised beds are a good way to grow vegetables and herbs. Railway sleepers (ties) can be used to create a low retaining wall. Their weight and stability make construction easy, and only minimal foundations are required.

1. Mark out the position of the bed with strings stretched between pegs, then fork over the ground in the bed to make sure of good drainage.

2. Make simple foundations for the walls by digging out a trench, 10cm (4in) deep and 10cm (4in) wider than the width of a sleeper (tie).

3. Fill the trench with hardcore and compact it firmly by tamping it down with a sledgehammer or heavy wooden post, leaving a surface that is level with the ground.

4. Position the first row of sleepers by centring them over the hardcore base, making sure that the corners form right angles. You can build the bed with one row of sleepers, as is shown here, or make the bed deeper.

5. Lay the second row on top, staggering the joints and corners like a brick bond. Ensure that the sides are level by using a straight edge.

6. Continue with the next row. If the bed is intended to go above three courses, drill vertical holes through the sleepers at the corner joints. Pass steel rods all the way through the sleepers and hammer firmly into the ground.

7. To give plants a really good start, fill the raised bed with new topsoil and dig in a thick layer of well-rotted organic manure, which can be obtained from a stable yard. Never use fresh manure, because this will create too much nitrogen as it breaks down, damaging the plants. If the manure is fresh, prepare the beds in autumn but do not plant anything until spring, when the manure will be well rotted. Alternatively, use potting mix made at home from vegetable waste.

above Rosemary (Rosmarinus officinalis) has pungent foliage that is a must in a potager garden.

Calendula officinalis

plant list

 1 *Dicksonia antarctica*
 2 *Lavandula angustifolia*
 3 *Rosmarinus officinalis*
 4 *Calendula officinalis*
 5 Silverbeet
 6 Tomatoes (*Lycopersicon esculentum*)
 7 Beetroot/beet (*Beta vulgaris*)
 8 Curly-leaved parsley (*Petroselinum crispum*)
 9 Flat-leaved parsley (*Petroselinum crispum*)
10 Rocket/arugula (*Eruca versicaria* subsp. *sativa*)
11 *Camellia* hedge

Timber pergola

Gravel pathway

above Tomatoes (Lycopersicon esculentum) are a good crop to grow in a small space.

right *Parsley (Petroselinum crispum) is perhaps the most used of all herbs. There are two forms – the curly leaved and the flat leaved. Curly-leaved parsley, shown here, is the more attractive and is often used for decoration and garnishes in cooking.*

left *Eruca versicaria subsp. sativa, or rocket (arugula), has a strong, mustard-like taste. This pungent herb lends interest to lettuce and other bland-tasting leaves as a salad ingredient. The centres of the small, white flowers are streaked with violet.*

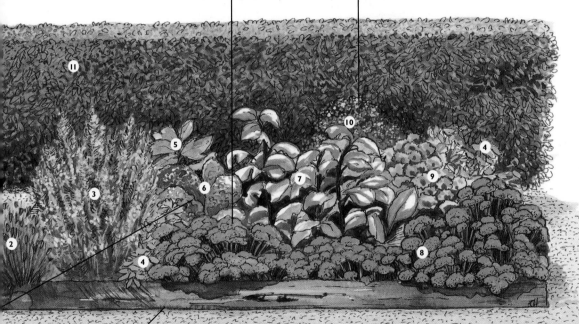

left *A raised bed means that you can import topsoil if the soil in your courtyard is not suitable for growing vegetables and herbs. The best soil in which to grow vegetables is slightly on the acid side of neutral. You can grow a wide variety of produce even in a small bed such as this.*

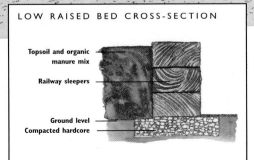

LOW RAISED BED CROSS-SECTION

Topsoil and organic manure mix

Railway sleepers

Ground level
Compacted hardcore

The clutter of modern life, the noise and frenetic activity leave us with a need for peace and tranquillity, which is well served by the soothing colours, gentle planting and informal design of the contemplative retreat. A successful courtyard haven will provide spiritual nourishment as well as physical relaxation, allowing you the time to contemplate and reflect. It will also help you to truly appreciate the cycle of nature as the seasons unfold to reveal flowers, fruits and seeds. Nurturing the soil and its plants is part of this healing process, refreshing your spirits and calming your mind.

CONTEMPLATIVE
retreats

A courtyard for contemplation should feel natural and understated, ordered but in a meandering fashion. It is not just for looking at, but should draw you in mentally and physically, inviting sensual discovery and providing a place to lose yourself among the sounds of breeze-rustled foliage, trickling water and birdsong. Water in the courtyard never fails to invigorate both mind and body. It provides a cool, clear space for reflecting forms in a surface lit with glints of sunlight, while attracting wildlife to drink and bathe.

Lush greenery brings life-giving moisture and oxygen to an urban atmosphere, restoring energy and a sense of wellbeing. A generous, graceful planting, mixing sculptural evergreens with deciduous shrubs and trees, will form a miniature landscape to reflect the changing seasons, from delicate spring blossom to fiery

autumn tints. To enable you to appreciate the results, provide comfortable seats at advantageous viewpoints for silent retreat from worldly cares. Paths and structures should blend sympathetically with the natural approach to planting and design, being made from textural and sensuous raw materials such as wood and stone, used in a form that is as close to their natural state as possible.

The lush, sculptural planting in a contemplative courtyard is also an excellent way to maintain a sense of privacy – a rare asset in an urban environment. A courtyard in the centre of a building would guarantee seclusion, with all the rooms looking inward on to a tranquil space, planted perhaps with bamboos, and with low benches around a carp-filled pool. You could extend the possibilities of the courtyard in winter by partly covering the courtyard with a sliding glass roof.

opposite *Panels of cut bamboo canes create an effective, but natural, screen.*
below *This serene "viewing garden", enclosed by dense thickets of bamboo, is informed by the Zen traditions of landscape imagery. Specially selected boulders are placed to represent islands within a raked stone "seascape".*
previous page *Tall tree ferns cast dappled shade, while also creating a sense of seclusion.*

gardens for viewing

Traditional Japanese temple gardens can teach us a lot about calm and stillness, our relationship with the natural world and the value of contemplation. Their approach to garden design differs significantly from that of the West, because gardens appear to emerge organically from the landscape, rather than being imposed superficially upon it. A reverence for nature is demonstrated in the tender way in which trees are nurtured and protected, especially when they are old or fragile.

Small, focused "viewing gardens" are set around the perimeter of temple buildings. Arranged as symbolic landscapes, these gardens invoke "nature as art" by reinterpreting the landscape in miniature form, using sculpted trees and specially placed rocks set in terrains of moss, gravel and water. In effect, travelling is experienced by remaining still, in contemplation of symbolic representations of mountains, rivers and seas.

Enclosed by low walls, these gardens are designed to be admired from a veranda or terrace. They number among them the famous Zen stone and sand gardens, though other, more naturalistic, rock and water gardens are just as frequently encountered. The viewing garden can be adapted to suit the Western courtyard, creating an intimate garden scene to be enjoyed both from a terrace and from inside the house. For year-round benefit, the arrangement works best if the courtyard is accessed through large French windows or sliding plate-glass doors to achieve an uninterrupted visual passage between inside and outside, with the windows acting as a picture frame for the garden image beyond.

> The composition of the "viewing garden" is arranged to interpret the **landscape** in an artful way.

left *Lichen-encrusted boulders dominate this miniature landscape, suggesting hills in a verdant plain, through which flows a "dry" river. Enclosure is provided by a fringe of red Acer palmatum against a boundary of bamboo canes.*
opposite *Attention in this courtyard is drawn to a dynamic central pool of moving water. Heavy wooden planks provide a visual and physical link to the perimeter path of stones.*

This intimate relationship with nature makes the courtyard a true outdoor room, allowing the seasonal qualities of light and energy to be enjoyed throughout the year. In summer, the space can be entirely opened up to create a seamless flow between indoors and outdoors.

The viewing garden should reflect the qualities of natural form and composition, rather than the traditional concept of Western formality, which is based upon rectangles and parallel lines. You should think instead of triangles, and concentrate on achieving asymmetric balance by visually weighting tall against low, and heavy against light. A tall *Trachycarpus* palm on one side of the courtyard, for example, would be balanced by a group of three rocks of differing sizes on the other. All groupings, whether of plants or decorative objects such as stones, should be arranged in threes or other odd numbers, depending on their size and spread. Paths should curve and meander, or turn at right angles, so as to obscure their destination from direct view.

If you have a view from above, an enclosed courtyard can present a dramatically textured pattern of plant shapes and colours, making viewing the courtyard from upstairs windows an exciting secondary experience to the view to be enjoyed from the ground. From this perspective, the horizontal plane of both plants and features takes on a new significance, encouraging the use of sweeping drifts of planting accented by the spreading leaf canopies of tree ferns and palm trees, set against a backdrop of pools and textured ground surface finishes.

Evolving through severe restrictions on living space, the courtyard concept that has featured for centuries in Japanese urban design lends itself readily to contemporary interpretation in the West. Apartments with tiny outdoor spaces at ground or basement level and terraced houses with shady, narrow side passages all have the potential to create miniature viewing gardens.

With some imagination, even gloomy basement rooms can be opened up to the outdoors to link with an otherwise unpromising area or light well. Picture windows can be installed, allowing rooms to be filled with natural light by day, while they are backlit by an illuminated courtyard at night. Such a small space would benefit from a truly minimal approach in planting and decoration, perhaps paved and dominated by a single specimen palm or clump of bamboo to throw shadows on the surrounding walls. A small pool with a fountain would introduce life and activity to complete the miniature stage set.

opposite *A meandering stream snakes slowly through this deeply green and tranquil Japanese-style courtyard where the only other colour permitted is that of the traditional red bridge. In place of moss, Soleirolia soleirolii spreads unchecked, while miniature conifers set among rocks give vertical interest.*

right *The massed effect of exotic planting brings a spirit of jungle adventure to this narrow courtyard. The eye is drawn along the path past pots of blue and white agapanthus.*

natural materials

above left *A wild-looking rock contrasts well with the fine, smooth, green foliage of Soleirolia soleirolii.*

above centre *A crushed slate path meanders like a dry river through the green landscape.*

above right *The dark leaves of* Ophiopogon planiscapus *'Nigrescens' emerge through differently shaped and textured shingle, cobbles and smoothly ground spheres.*

In keeping with the philosophy of being at one with the natural environment, it is important to choose construction materials that are in as natural a state as possible, rather than manufactured materials such as brick or concrete. Softly textured boundaries can be created with screens of pale bamboo or reeds, while a darker effect can be achieved by using panels of woven willow or heather.

Paving materials with a riven surface have an appropriately textural appearance but need to have their crisp edges broken by flowing groups of clump-forming and spreading plants. Paths with a loose structural character are visually sympathetic to their surroundings, and crushed flakes of silvery slate give a sense of movement, rather like a flowing stream, enhanced by a pleasant crunchy sound and feel underfoot.

Gravel chips and pea shingle are readily available at a fairly low cost, though they can look a little harsh. Smooth, washed beach pebbles are a much more attractive alternative, with colours varying in tone from creamy white through pinkish grey to brownish black. Pebbles are available in sizes graded from a few millimetres, perfect for paths, to more generously proportioned cobbles from which decorative terraces and naturalistic water features can be created.

In order to achieve a comfortable visual balance, you will find that even the smallest courtyard can benefit from a clear area on which to rest the eye. In a conventional garden, this function is usually filled by a lawn, but within an Oriental interpretation, an area of pebbles can have the same calming effect. To avoid the possibility

of lifelessness, a curving design can be raked into the surface to add visual interest, suggesting an undulating landscape or the ripples of the sea. Large, well-shaped boulders can be selected individually and placed to create a dramatically graphic statement, suggesting floating islands or natural crags.

A purist Zen gravel garden can seem unresponsive to Western eyes, so it may be a good idea to introduce clumps of moss or tufted festuca and sedge grasses to bring fresh, vegetative relief. To retain the original concept, however, use them as focus accents rather than spreading them liberally around. Small trees, such as *Acer palmatum* var. *dissectum* and flowering cherries (*Prunus*), often have beautiful bark as well as delightful foliage and spring blossom, so these would also be suitable for enlivening a gravel garden, especially when grown near to paths, where some moss can gently break the edges.

Rustic steps are a good way to accommodate changes of level. Reclaimed hardwood railway sleepers (ties) or sawn logs make effective risers, retaining steps dressed with pebbles or slate. Small evergreen *Polystichum* ferns can create a delicate liasion with surrounding planting by foiling any hard edges with their curling fronds.

The soft characteristics of untreated wood fit well in a rusticated landscape, and decking can be used to create a raised level where required. A decking terrace leading from the house would make an excellent viewing platform from which to gain an overview of the whole courtyard, while a narrow strip of decking could traverse or edge an informal wildlife pond.

above left *A fine bamboo window blind, fixed high in a wisteria, becomes an effective outdoor sunscreen.*
above right *This smooth glass cobble creates a reflective highlight among pieces of dark granite.*

water features

opposite top *With its curved decking paths and central fountain, this adventurous design looks like a cool aquatic "eye". The energy of the water spout, which forces its way up through a mesh-encased cube of crushed glass, contrasts well with the tranquillity of the still pool below.*

above right *Aquatic plants lurk intriguingly in this upturned glass fish bowl.*

below *A tsukubai creates a charming effect by a terrace that is edged with cobbles and pebbles. Birds will come to enjoy some cool refreshment.*

A naturalistic courtyard is greatly enhanced by water, introducing a range of sensory qualities, such as reflected light and sound. The choice of water feature – whether it is to be a pool or rill, or a more modest bowl or container – will depend on the space available and the emphasis the feature is to have in the design. Of course, complicated devices are not prerequisites for style, and when space or resources are limited, simple water features are perfect. A shallow bowl with a perching rim, for example, will attract birds, while a deep stone basin with a ladle gives visitors the chance to wash on a hot day.

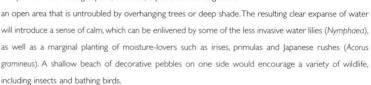

If you do have enough space, however, a pond can be dug out of an open area that is untroubled by overhanging trees or deep shade. The resulting clear expanse of water will introduce a sense of calm, which can be enlivened by some of the less invasive water lilies (*Nymphaea*), as well as a marginal planting of moisture-lovers such as irises, primulas and Japanese rushes (*Acorus gramineus*). A shallow beach of decorative pebbles on one side would encourage a variety of wildlife, including insects and bathing birds.

Such a pool would combine well with a decking platform or canopied veranda, with benches set for relaxation and stone jars planted with waterside grasses, arum lilies (*Zantedeschia*) or glaucous hostas. To fit cohesively with the natural look, the platform or veranda should be constructed from bold, natural hardwood in a simple design that blends with the landscape.

You can introduce movement to the pool by installing a submersible pump that drives the water in a circular motion around the pool edge. Alternatively, it can be positioned to produce a series of low, bubbling spouts among the pebbles on a shallow beach at the water's edge. A simple planting of reeds, able to cope with the water disturbance, would be appropriate here (water lilies prefer still water).

A cascade would also not be out of place with such a pond, and the spoil resulting from the pond excavation could create the hill for the cascade's foundation. Carefully placed boulders and large stones, with dwarf shrubs, ferns and mosses growing among them in a naturalistic way, will make a miniature landscape to carry the pumped cascade, similar to those found in traditional Japanese viewing gardens.

Streams and rills can be used to bisect a courtyard, while a still canal, edged with paving, can create space among planting beds, making a pleasant resting place for the eye. Less formally, water may be pumped along a shallow, snaking channel over a bed of stones to create a gentle, rippling sound.

left *A tranquil pool of still water, encased by a curving zinc container, is emphasized by a bed of dark pebbles and border of burgundy tolmeia. It is brilliantly highlighted by the lime-green foliage in the foreground and the soft mounds of box beyond.*

contemplative planting

above left *This path-side grouping provides an interesting contrast of textures and forms.*
above centre *Evoking a Buddhist temple garden, these white and pink lotus flowers float surreally above the broad, saucer-like leaves.*
above right *The sculptural profile of this slow-growing pine makes it perfect for a specimen feature.*

Japanese designers often use plants and materials symbolically, either to give the garden a spiritual dimension or to recreate a landscape in miniature, a concept that is well suited to the urban plot. The evergreen pine tree, for example, is revered as a symbol of stability and endurance. The Japanese black pine (*Pinus thunbergii*) and red pine (*P. densiflora*) are both available in dwarf cultivars and will take a lot of training and pruning. Prostrate and pendulous forms of pines, such as *Pinus strobus* 'Nana' and *P. densiflora* 'Pendula', are ideal for sculpted courtyards, particularly in conjunction with gravel and rock areas. Suitably sculptural subjects can also be found among other conifers, with the spruces (*Picea*) offering attractive dwarf forms.

Dramatic sculptural form can also be provided by the New Zealand tree fern (*Dicksonia antarctica*), with its strong, fibrous trunk and broad canopy of fresh green fronds. Although considered tender, these ferns frequently flourish in the shelter of a courtyard. If suitable conditions do not prevail, the Chinese fan palm (*Trachycarpus fortunei*) and the Mediterranean fan palm (*Chamaerops humilis*) will provide a similar effect.

A contemplative courtyard needs a strong base of evergreens to maintain its appearance throughout the year, but a selection of deciduous species will reflect the changing seasons. Nothing represents the transition from winter to spring as aptly as the cherry blossom (*Prunus*). Just one small tree, such as pure white 'Shirotae', deep pink 'Cheal's Weeping' or scented, shell-pink 'Takasago', is enough to restore the

spirits. Space should also be found for at least one elegant camellia, which offers both evergreen structure and beautiful white, pink or red flowers in spring. Dwarf rhododendrons and evergreen azaleas also provide a kaleidoscope of late-spring, often fragrant, flowers. Autumn is the other transitional period in the garden, when the brilliant maples (*Acer*) come into their own, the delicate, deeply lobed foliage of *A. palmatum* turning from bright green in spring to delicious tones of yellow, gold and red as summer ends.

Plants that shiver in the breeze, creating dappled sunlight and evoking the sights and sounds of the country, are also ideal for a contemplative courtyard. Statuesque bamboos, with their narrow stems and clattering leaves, make handsome screens for boundaries and paths, as do clumps of fine-leaved grasses. Bamboo can be very invasive, though, and the *Pleioblastus* group should be avoided in a restricted space or confined to pots. The *Phyllostachys* genus is more suitable, containing some of the most handsome bamboos, including the prized black bamboo (*P. nigra*), golden *P. aurea* and slender *P. flexuosa*.

Among the medium to tall grasses, *Miscanthus sinensis* offers some of the most beautiful specimens, with lovely foliage and silvery flowerheads; stripy 'Zebrinus', elegant 'Gracillimus' and arching 'Kleine Fontäne' are just a few examples. For contrast, the low, round tufts of *Festuca glauca* cultivars, with their fine, blue-grey leaves, make elegant focal points when grouped together in a sunny spot.

above left *The graceful fronds of the New Zealand tree fern* (Dicksonia antarctica) *wave above the stout fibrous trunk to create a handsome feature for a sheltered courtyard.*
above right *The simplicity of this massed planting of spiky blue iris backed by the arching fronds of pale green ferns contributes to the tranquillity of the scene.*

CASE STUDY

peaceful retreat

A thoughtful approach to balance and harmony in this city garden has resulted in a haven that pleases all the senses, perfect for its owner, a practitioner of complementary medicine. The sensitive, holistic design interprets the opposing forces of yin and yang, while reflecting five elements – metal, fire, earth, air and water – in the materials used in the construction of the garden, as well as in the colours of the planting.

A high terrace leading from the house provides a west-facing platform from which to view the overall scene, with a black metal table and chairs positioned on the paving to take full advantage of summer sunsets. Steps descend to a slate path that divides the energetic, south-facing yang side of the garden, with its hot and fiery planting, from the cool yin subjects languishing quietly opposite. The whole effect is one of calm tranquillity and harmony.

The path, which turns at right angles to create an indirect route through the garden, leads to a quiet pool traversed by stepping stones. The pool is watched over by a contemplative buddha who sits calmly in front of a thin mirror that rests informally against the wall.

The meandering journey taken by the path keeps the visitor guessing at what will be around the next corner, thus giving the garden an element of mystery. A thick screen of rustling bamboo obscures the bottom of the garden completely from view. The path eventually culminates in a secret woodland glade with a rewarding bamboo deckchair in which to rest and recuperate. Dividing the garden into clearly defined sections is an excellent way of disguising a long, narrow garden plot.

above *Spiky, energetic forms add height and drama to the hot yang border.*
above left *A flaring torch light positioned at the edge of a path is ideal for lighting the way through a thickly planted courtyard.*
left *The symbolic planting in this courtyard is designed to reflect the opposing forces of yin and yang. The power of yang is represented by the vibrant colours of the planting in this bed.*
opposite *The paved area at the top of the courtyard provides a vantage point from which to view the contrasting planting beds.*

THE GARDEN PLAN

laying a slate path

A slate path makes for an atmospheric garden, with a strong emphasis on natural harmony and organic materials. It is also satisfyingly crunchy underfoot.

1. Mark out the area of the path with strings stretched between pegs, then dig it out to a depth of at least 30cm (12in).
2. Compact the surface thoroughly by tamping it down with a stout wooden post or garden roller.
3. Lay hardcore to a depth of 15cm (6in). At the same time, set preserved wooden edging boards along both sides of the path, over a thin layer of hardcore, so that the boards finish at about 2.5cm (1in) above the adjacent ground level. Compact as above. The edging boards are approximately 30cm (12in) deep and 2.5cm (1in) wide.
4. Spread a layer of coarse gravel to a depth of 5cm (2in) and roll or firm it by treading firmly all over it.
5. Cover this with a layer of finely sifted gravel, 5cm (2in) thick, and rake it level.
6. Finally, cover the fine gravel with slate chippings, taking the path up to the level of the ground surface. Soak the path with a hose to bind the fine gravel and wash away the dust.

Melianthus major

plant list

 1 *Typha minima*
 2 *Holboellia latifolia*
 3 *Euphorbia mellifera*
 4 *Phormium tenax*
 5 *Dodonaea viscosa* 'Purpurea'
 6 *Trachycarpus fortuneii*
 7 *Sophora microphylla*
 8 *Cordyline australis*
 9 *Yucca rostrata*
10 *Albizia julibrissin* 'Rosea'
11 *Iris confusa*
12 *Yucca* species
13 *Astelia chathamica*
14 *Beschorneria yuccoides*
15 *Festuca glauca*
16 *Agapanthus africanus*
17 *Crocosmia* 'Solfaterre'
18 *Melianthus major*
19 *Euphorbia amygdaloides* 'Purpurea'
20 *Canna* 'Durban'
21 *Musa basjoo*
22 *Polystichum setiferum* 'Divisilobum'

below *The still surface of this pool is perfect for reflecting the gently rustling foliage of this garden. Its ebony depths are entirely fitting.*

Fence

Grey Snowdonian slate

Pool

Stepping stones

Timber edging

Brick wall

11

11

10

6

6

8

8

7

18

9

17

12

13

Irish limestone flags

16

15

14

13

16

Row of bamboos

8

22

6

21

8

above *This corner at the top of the garden is a perfect spot from which to view the tranquil scene.*

SLATE PATH CROSS-SECTION

slate chippings

Timber edging board, 30 x 2.5cm (12 x 1in)

5cm (2in) finely sifted gravel

5cm (2in) coarse gravel

15cm (6in) hardcore

above *Slate is a wonderfully natural material for laying a path through this contemplative retreat.*

The effect of pressure of time and space on
modern living has altered our perception of leisure
and relaxation for ever, and this is reflected in
today's domestic architecture as well as the design
of the contemporary courtyard, with its clean lines,
low-maintenance approach and structural planting
that demands the minimum of care.

The contemporary courtyard can also be
a stimulating setting for entertaining as well as a
showcase for avant-garde design, with its fascinating
use of brightly coloured hard landscaping, modern
sculpture and dramatic water features.

CONTEMPORARY

spaces

Some contemporary garden designers concentrate on hard landscaping, creating courtyards that are clean, crisp and minimal. While this can be refreshing, it is important to remember the part that plants can play. Even in a totally formal space, with clean architectural lines, there is no need to do away with the colour, movement and texture that are provided by plants, or, indeed, a sense of fun.

Today's new construction materials and the use of bold, brilliant colours and strange textures have turned many traditional gardening ideas on their head, where coloured glass pretends to be planting and paving is employed to play visual tricks. For example, a water sculpture created from glass or reflective polished steel may flash in the sunlight and then glow at night under carefully positioned floodlighting.

The modern courtyard also allows the urban dweller to have fun with a quirky selection of containers and associated planting, as well as in the choice of cutting-edge sculpture. Choosing intriguing, abstract pieces of art made from unusual materials brings a whole new dimension to the design of a courtyard, allowing for the expression of personal tastes and preferences.

Low maintenance is also an important factor in the contemporary courtyard, with an emphasis on hard surfaces that can be brushed or hosed down easily. Similar principles apply to the planting, with structural evergreens being the best choice because they are easy to look after. While the evergreens can form the framework of the planting, textural perennials can be used to fill in the spaces during their season of glory.

opposite *A low wooden table echoes the eccentric shape of the pool beyond.*
below *In this courtyard, huge open screens frame the area like the walls of a giant aquarium filled with clusters of sea birds and tropical fish. Low wooden benches hug the perimeter walls, with the pool and spa left exposed to the sun.*
previous page *This design uses strong colour contrasts and geometry for its bold effect.*

avant-garde design

The approach to modern courtyard design ensures that bold geometry of form, smooth textures and clean planting combine to create gardens with a dynamic structure and character. The design of a contemporary courtyard should appear as an uninterrupted flow from the house, reflecting its architecture, scale and form. It should echo the appearance of the building, creating visual and physical links between the house and the hard landscaping. Features and elements in the courtyard can also be used to mirror the shape of a window, the height of a door or the style of a roof line to create a complementary outdoor reflection.

Less is definitely more in the modern courtyard, which uses **white space** to emphasize features and focal points.

Wide, uncluttered terraces combined with sequential rectangular blocks of low monochrome planting will help to create a feeling of freedom and airiness. Plants can be set in the earth at ground level or in raised beds that are formed by smooth-cast retaining walls. These "quiet" spaces are balanced by physical and visual separations and transitions to introduce a sense of movement that can be experienced while passing through the courtyard.

above *Bold cacti and succulents form the focus of the planting in this desert-style courtyard.*
right *This unusual courtyard, which is designed to look like the sea as it gently laps the shore, epitomizes the vibrancy of today's garden design. The blue crushed glass seems to reflect the sky, while white-painted raised beds are filled with brightly coloured perennials and structural evergreens.*

Creating spatial divisions to provide focus and contrast is necessary throughout the design. The water canal is a versatile device for creating separation, reversing the role of a path and contrasting in texture and spirit with hard paving and plants. It can play a pivotal linking role, forging a connection between the house and a boundary, from where it can emerge as a cascade from the wall, or flow through a series of channels with tiny spill-overs at changes of ground level.

Overhead structures create three-dimensional statements that can link with the architectural features of the house, while also accentuating the shapes of the ground layout. A bold steel pergola, designed to echo a window line, will draw the eye and emphasize a route, while the shadows it casts add to the dynamic effect as they change shape and direction during the day.

A contemporary courtyard makes a cool, understated vehicle for sculptural statement, creating almost a gallery theatre. Free-standing screens formed from metal or concrete painted in brilliant colours make dashing spatial divisions or backdrops for planting. A series of mirrored obelisks would introduce additional light in a shady area, together with an illusion of space through their multifaceted reflective surfaces.

opposite left *Blocks of glossy black ophiopogon and dark green mondo grass are punctuated by sculptural clumps of toning bromeliads in a tropical border.*

opposite right *Low ground-cover plants can be used effectively as living mosaic. Here, rectangular blocks of single-species planting, in contrasting tones of green, black and grey, replicate the decorative panels and stained-glass screen of the walls.*

left *Gigantic roof timbers have been set on end to screen and frame a narrow gravel path. This is inset with slim wooden slats that repeat the rhythm of the vertical timbers. The colourful underplanting of bright cerise cosmos presents a naïve complement to the massive structures above.*

above *A curvaceous, stainless-steel screen, laser-cut with leaf motifs, makes an arresting modern backdrop to groups of softly flowering perennials.*

funky materials

Hard landscaping plays a significant part in the modern courtyard, and the choice of materials that is now deemed acceptable has changed many preconceptions about garden style. Industrial materials like stainless-steel reinforcing mesh and concrete are now finding new uses in the home and garden, as are coloured Perspex (Plexiglas), fabrics and crushed glass. Colour produces a surreal effect in translucent materials, its intensity changing under different lighting conditions. Perspex is a tough, lightweight material available in sheet form in boiled-sweet colours. A screen composed of different coloured panels can take on the look of a Mondrian painting, while throwing a cast of colour across its surroundings. Orange, red and yellow give a cheerful sunny effect, while blues and greens tend to be somewhat eerie.

Glass also has a place in the modern courtyard garden. A screen of thick glass bricks provides a solid backdrop while allowing light to pass through. Glass bricks can also be used for part of a boundary wall, to admit light with no loss of privacy. Glass aggregates can be used for special-effect ground cover where there will be no foot traffic. In crushed form, it can be raked for a Zen-style garden. By contrast, a sea of shiny dark pebbles makes an exotic backdrop for spiny, blue-grey agaves or other succulents.

Concrete is probably the most versatile building material in existence, its strength, combined with plasticity, allowing it to be formed and finished in a multitude of ways. The sophisticated decorative results that can be achieved are a far cry from the crude grey industrial concrete so often encountered elsewhere.

In a courtyard design, concrete is likely to be used in retaining walls for planting beds and pools, but it can also be formed into curvaceous furniture and planters. It is usually poured into a mould *in situ*, though where a very fine finish or unusual shape is required, it may be pre-cast off site, resulting in inevitable weight and handling considerations.

Concrete can also be made into free-standing features like screens and archways. A free-standing solid concrete screen can serve as a backdrop for a water cascade or a sculpture, but, if

opposite *This surreal design relies on illusion and colour for its effect. Vertical panels of Perspex form the backdrop to a rectilinear layout of beds. Three* Ligustrum ionandrum *stand sentinel over the area.*

left *Diminutive grey succulents are planted in a bed of broken turquoise shells.*

below *Panels of coloured Perspex wired between horizontal rails create an effective punctuated screen.*

pierced by a round or square shape, creates an unexpected peephole to a separate part of the courtyard.

Cement can also play a part in the courtyard if you want an absolutely smooth, clean and elegant surface. Pure white cement makes a more refreshing alternative to the normal dull grey, or colour pigments can be added to make a strong contrasting statement; even gold leaf can be used. If you prefer a more raunchy effect, textured aggregates such as polished pebbles or glass nuggets can be incorporated into the mix or laid on the surface after pouring. The surplus cement is then brushed off to expose the granular material. When cement is poured into a mould of wooden shuttering planks, the wood grain is shown in relief on the hardened cement. Another way to create a *faux* wood-grain finish is to brush or score the surface of the cement when it has nearly set.

Mirror is an exceptionally useful illusionary tool in a courtyard, reflecting light into a shady area or multiplying images to give a false idea of space. Where there is an attractive feature or façade, it can be set into an opposite wall to create a double image or, more inventively, it can be formed into tall, free-standing columns or panels set in series among low planting. These combine sculptural and spatial roles, both reflecting the surroundings and apparently extending the size of the courtyard.

Stainless-steel sheet can be polished to an almost mirror-like shine and used to reflect light. It is particularly useful in diffusing the effect of an overshadowing building or large tree. When creating a screen or boundary, shapes can be cut out by laser to let through light and external views. Textured embossed finishes can be used to make stylized slip-resistant pathways and steps with a somewhat industrial look.

above *Tiny grey succulents are fixed like corsage flowers in a screen made from sisal rope.*
left *Fine textile panels, held taut by thin battens at the top and bottom, provide shade without totally obscuring the light and the view.*
opposite *This modern interpretation of the stained-glass window has a dynamic physical role, bisecting the courtyard into two distinct areas. A narrow slot provides a glimpse of the screened seating area beyond the border of colourful perennials and grasses.*

modern containers

above left *A generously proportioned zinc container sets off a diminutive planting of fragrant, grey-leaved thyme.*
above centre *Upright acorus grass emerges from a vivid blue-painted pot, clad with dyed seashells of a deeper tone.*
above right *The smoothly rounded curves of this terracotta bowl provide a gentle resting place for an architectural succulent.*

A courtyard garden is often highly dependent on containers, due to the restricted space or lack of ground soil, and in high-level projects like balconies and roof terraces all the planting has, of necessity, to be in containers. To keep the plants healthy, you will need plenty of potting mix and either a dedicated waterer or an automatic irrigation system.

To complete the pared-down, minimalist look of a courtyard that goes with contemporary building styles, cleaner lines should replace the often highly decorated traditional planters. New shapes have developed in two particular ways. One is the trend to draw the sloping, round flowerpot shape upward, resulting in a tall, narrow planter with a height greater than its diameter. This form is usually made from terracotta or stoneware, though metal versions do exist. It is extremely elegant, though its narrowness renders it a little unstable in exposed situations. Low-growing plants or clipped domed shapes work best visually in these pots; they also balance the oversized base and have less of a tendency to catch the wind.

The other development is the vertical-sided container. From a desire to do something different and bring an instant new look to town gardens, the shiny zinc tub emerged. This vertical-sided round shape gained instant popularity because it was easy to make from sheet metal, though its proportions are critical if an unflattering "blobby" effect is to be avoided. Thin metal planters are, however, unsuitable for healthy cultivation, since they have a propensity to overheat in direct sunshine, risking damage to roots and

dehydration. The answer to this problem was the development of a range of sophisticated zinc planters that are constructed with a double skin to create an insulating air space that protects the soil from heat. The smoky grey, patinated finish has the look of lead, without its unmanageable weight. Proportions are balanced, with cubes and oversized columns that can be organized into multifaceted groups of differing heights, ideal for restricted terrace areas. There are also elegant, sloping-sided round and square forms, including specimen planters up to 1.2m (4ft) high.

Sheet zinc is more suitable as an excellent finishing medium over a custom-made wooden form, achieving a high-tech look for a system of built-in planting beds, which may, for example, be used on a roof terrace where weight is a consideration. Zinc will dull down over time, so if a permanent shiny finish is needed, the only option is to use stainless steel, which, though extremely expensive, will seldom deteriorate.

It is always best to use materials for their inherent character, rather than trying to reproduce a copy in fibreglass, which invariably lacks the integrity of the original. Just as Perspex (Plexiglas) screens do not pretend to be glass, the latest polyester planters are unashamedly themselves. These lightweight cube forms might be the new modern classics, however. They come in various bright colours that will not fade, as they are resistant to ultraviolet light, while their slight translucency also creates the possibility of incorporating lighting effects within a planted group.

above left *The exquisite form of this textural glazed jar needs no further adornment.*
above centre *Lightweight galvanized planters are ideal for planting on roof terraces.*
above right *Fine-leaved black ophiopogon provides a subtle foil for this retro terrazzo pot.*

contemporary sculpture

right *A gentle stone mask lends serenity to this quiet, grass-filled bed.*
opposite *An ephemeral screen has been created from clear Perspex (Plexiglas) floats that are strung on nylon cords between fine metal rails.*
below *A row of massive wooden columns forms a dynamic sculptural feature that is simple, yet relatively inexpensive, to construct.*

The clean, cool space of a modern courtyard can be seen as an outdoor gallery, providing a perfect backdrop for contemporary sculpture. The courtyard space is equally appropriate for displaying a single piece of sculpture or for staging a large collection of different pieces. The salient difference from an interior space is that, in a natural environment, you will need to consider the metaphysical character of the work in relation to your surrounding landscape. A piece of stone, for example, when carved and polished to expose its ancient strata lines and colour, becomes an evocative and sensual form – a solid piece that connects to its origins buried deep below the ground. Wood, too, has a powerful connection with the natural world: once rooted in the earth, it now exposes its interior secrets under the carver's eye or perhaps stands aloof, its natural, uncarved form interpreted as abstract sculpture.

A construction that is formed from strands of wire has the effect of being light and air: it seems to drift on the wind, an ephemeral vision to be caught only by chance. Mirror glass possesses similarly elusive qualities. In the form of tall, free-standing panels, it can be used to clever effect by reflecting light and multiplying images to present a distracting and constantly changing series of images to the onlooker. A striking idea would be to position a tall series of mirror-glass panels to form the central feature and *raison d'être* of a small courtyard, catching the sun during the day, but with a ghostly metamorphosis at night under spotlights.

Light can be used to produce sculptural effects in its own right, and there are some new types of lighting now available that are rather exciting. Tiny fairy lights, for example, set into clear, flexible plastic tubes, make a versatile device that can be twined around trees or knotted into informal abstract sculptures, so creating a magical atmosphere, perfect for entertaining friends. Optical fibres can also be introduced to create interesting night-time effects. Loosely arranged, they will look like a sea of waving grasses tipped with tiny gleaming dots, while tied in clusters they resemble twinkling sea anemones.

fantastical water

Much of the emphasis of recent garden design has been on the creation of innovative water features, a bonus for makers of gardens, with ever more elaborate concepts being featured at gardening shows. Funnels and spouts vie with spinning crystal orbs, while shimmering towers of glass compete with pyramids of bright steel cushions, creating a pulsating flow of light and energy.

In hot climates, where life is spent out of doors, emphasis is placed firmly on the swimming pool, which often dominates the entire courtyard. Cooler zones need not miss out altogether, however, since conceptual ideas can be borrowed or adapted, and with global warming, plunge pools and jacuzzis may soon become a feature of every terrace.

The pool cascade, made famous by David Hockney, has remained in everyone's imagination and is an easy

> No self-respecting courtyard can be without a **sparkling** water feature, whether this is a gushing cascade or a water bowl.

technique to adapt to a small area. Water pumped up behind a false wall is released in a forceful gush through a slot into a pool below, creating dancing lights and shadows on its moving surface. As an alternative, you could replace the pool with a thick bed of glass pebbles, preferably lit from below for a dramatic night-time glow.

above *Water flows and gushes through a concentric arrangement of steel slots, which are set with gleaming plates of translucent glass. The effect is one of movement and reflected light.*
opposite *This immaculately designed, sky-high spa invites you to enter its warm, calming depths.*

A chaotic water effect is not always desirable in a courtyard, where noise can echo and reverberate. Using the same basic system as the pool cascade, a gentle fall can be achieved if water is released in a broad sweep along the top edge of a wall, to flow down closely over the surface. This idea translates well to a free-standing screen made of polished steel, transparent glass or, for greater texture, a concrete wall painted with shimmering gold. Water can also transform a polished steel monolith into a floating mirror, as it slips surreptitiously over its surface.

Water looks especially optimistic when it is pushing upward, and some of the most interesting fountains operate without a visible water supply. Narrow columns of water shooting out of the paving are amusing to look at (and fun to jump among), especially when the water spouts up in alternating sequences of low and high pressure.

For those with calmer tastes, a formal pool makes a tranquil focal point and place for contemplation, well suited to the architectural constraints of the courtyard. No adornment is needed, save perhaps a few fish to glitter in the sunlight, and a seating ledge around the perimeter is useful. Quiet water can be used spatially to dissect an area. Tiny pools connected by narrow canals set flush with the paving create a sense of passage through the courtyard. A pump set to bubble water over a flat stone in each pool will generate a gentle flow, cutting through the space like a geometric ribbon. This is especially effective when traversing a series of shallow changes of level.

structural planting

Geometry is an important design factor in a modern courtyard or terrace, and it can be achieved not only through the hard landscaping surfaces and structures but also through the planting. The clean, simple lines of a minimalist design can be reinforced by structuring the planting to follow the walls and paths, set in architectural blocks that lie at ground level or perhaps in a sequence of raised beds which are stepped in terraces.

By using foliage plants of differing form and habit, colour and texture, it is possible to create a range of adventurous optical effects that echo the architectural features of the courtyard design. Chequerboard and striped effects work well at ground level, where they can easily be seen from above, while repeating plants can be employed as screens and path borders.

Mat-spreading and mound- or tuft-forming evergreens make the best choice of plants for low-level work, with grey and lime, purple and black being the most effective colours. Good texture is also important. The black, blade-like foliage of *Ophiopogon planiscapus* 'Nigrescens', for example, makes a gleaming, faintly sinister statement, while, in contrast, the needle-fine, grey-tufted grass *Festuca glauca* has a light and airy sophistication. Ground-hugging succulents, such as the rosette-forming *Sempervivum* group and some of the fleshy sedums, can be used to provide an exotic effect, and all can work well if planted in conjunction with a mineral mulch. Indeed, the foliage colours, which vary from silver-grey through to reddish-purple, are set off beautifully by a textured mulch such as white marble chippings, mauve slate or dark, polished river pebbles.

Small shrubs, like fragrant, silvery santolinas and lavenders, respond well to being clipped into tight shapes, while larger-growing box (*Buxus sempervirens*) and yew (*Taxus baccata*) make good dark green alternatives with screening potential. They can be trained into blocks or, if shaped into spheres, may be set in rows within a rectangular template. Shorter, spreading bamboos lend themselves to block planting and creating low barriers. *Pleioblastus variegatus*, with its white-striped foliage, and white-edged *Sasa veitchii* are both excellent candidates for this treatment.

As an alternative to a minimalist planting, a tropical treatment can act as a foil to the cool, clean lines of contemporary architecture, introducing an energetic visual experience composed of exotic flowers, spiky leaves and tall, bare trunks. Palms, agaves, yuccas, phormiums and cordylines, for example, all have the architectural strength to hold their own against a stark backdrop of bare walls and floors, and are best employed in bold planting groups to create an exhilarating theatre of shape and form. Their sunlit shadows will dance by day, while carefully placed lighting can further embolden them at night, throwing their dramatic silhouettes in bizarre patterns against walls and floors.

opposite above *Arum lilies majestically fill the space in this pale screen wall.*

opposite below *The bold forms of yuccas and cycads create a theatrical ambience in this densely packed courtyard.*

above *Tall, vertical trunks echo the form of the rustic pergola, while spiky, desert-style planting results in an energetic contrast with the pale, smooth background walls.*

left *A dynamic, spiny agave thrusts itself heavenward on this rooftop terrace.*

CASE STUDY

seashore chic

This exciting courtyard garden by the sea is the ultimate in sophistication and seclusion. The outstandingly beautiful view of the sea is complemented by the sympathetic seashore planting as well as by a design that includes pebbles, pools and comfortable loungers.

The terrace-level, floodlit swimming pool seems literally to emerge from beneath the house, from where it runs out to a pebble beach that is set with a collection of bubbling, geyser-style fountains and fringed by large boulders strewn among the tropical trees. Changes of level have been carved out of the site as it slopes down to the sea. These are accentuated by the cascades that run down to the rocky shallows below the sunken bar. This in turn serves the elegant pool-level spa from its high counter.

The clean and considered design, which has been executed with the highest quality construction materials and immaculate detailing, makes a cool and restrained foil for the dramatic planting of energetic, spiky forms. The courtyard becomes almost seamless with the shoreline beyond, while conserving a sense of privacy and its own distinctive character.

Great attention has been given to the design details. The elegant, black-and-white striped bar stools match the comfortable loungers on the upper terrace, while the architecture of the house blends easily with the colour and materials of the hard landscaping. A magnificent balcony, which resembles the prow of a ship as it carves a path through the ocean, jutts out of the upper terrace, affording a panoramic view of the courtyard and the surrounding area.

above *Crisp black and white loungers provide an ideal vantage point from which to view the courtyard and the seascape beyond.*
above left *The bubbling water spouts that are dotted among the cobbles and boulders echo the rushing of the ocean as it ebbs from the shore.*
left *An elegantly curved bar with high stools make this the perfect spot for informal seaside entertaining.*
opposite *The elegant pool, with its mirror-like surface, runs under the house, creating a smooth transition between the building and the courtyard.*

THE GARDEN PLAN

building a cobble fountain

A cobble fountain is an excellent way of introducing the sound of gushing water without installing a full-size fountain or stream. This courtyard contains a number of fountains.

above *The cobble fountains spray out from among the pebbles, echoing the splash of the waves on the distant shore.*

I. Choose a level site and clear an area of ground about 1.5m (5ft) in diameter. Dig a hole slightly larger than the diameter and depth of the plastic bin that will form the reservoir and put a shallow layer of sand over the base.

2. Place the bin in the hole and check the rim is level with the soil. If necessary, remove the bin and adjust the sand.

3. Fill in the gap around the bin with soil, ramming it down with a wooden post. Dig a saucer-like shape in the area around the bin, and rake out any stones. Remove any soil from the bin and wipe clean.

4. Place some bricks at the bottom of the bin and position the pump on top (this stops any debris from being sucked into the pump). Check that the rigid pipe for the fountain is 5–8cm (2–3in) higher than the sides of the bin. Fill with water.

5. Drape a circular plastic sheet, about 1.5m (5ft) in diameter, over the whole area and cut out a hole slightly wider than the fountain pipe, to allow the water to drain back into the bin. Position the sheet so that the pipe protrudes through the hole.

6. Place a strong piece of large galvanized mesh over the bin, then add a piece of smaller mesh on top of this. Make sure that the fountain pipe protrudes through both pieces of mesh.

7. Arrange a layer of cobbles over the surface and check that the height of the spout is working as desired. Complete the cobble design so that it obscures the plastic sheet and the mesh. Make sure that the switch to the pump cable is waterproof and meets all relevant safety standards.

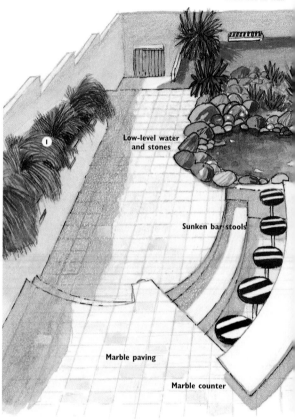

Low-level water and stones

Sunken bar stools

Marble paving

Marble counter

Carex flagellifera

plant list

I *Carex flagellifera*
2 *Selliera radicans*
3 *Festuca novae-zelandiae*
4 *Dracaena draco*
5 *Strelitzia juncea*

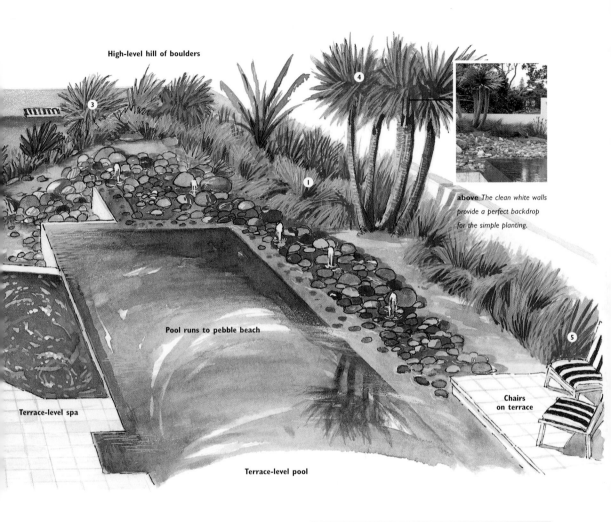

High-level hill of boulders

above *The clean white walls provide a perfect backdrop for the simple planting.*

Pool runs to pebble beach

Terrace-level spa

Chairs on terrace

Terrace-level pool

COBBLE FOUNTAIN CROSS-SECTION

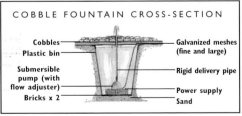

Cobbles

Plastic bin

Submersible pump (with flow adjuster)

Bricks x 2

Galvanized meshes (fine and large)

Rigid delivery pipe

Power supply

Sand

left *The cobble fountains appear at random throughout this seashore courtyard, bubbling up energetically between the pebbles.*

A courtyard garden is the epitome of the room outside. It is a complete space with a story to tell, and so you should try to create a design that is in sympathy with your home. Close attention to the character of the hard-landscaping materials as well as the quality of execution will pay off time and again, resulting in a courtyard that improves with maturity as weathering takes its natural toll.

This gallery focuses in more detail on aspects of construction, enabling you to make informed decisions about the best ways to give personality and style to your design.

PRACTICAL
focus

floors and surfaces

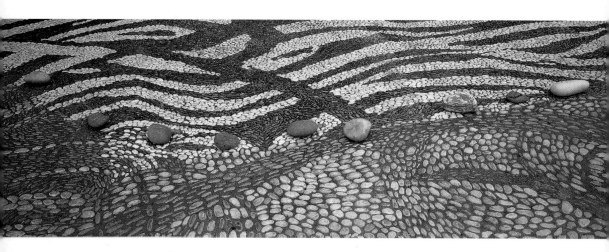

above *Informal materials such as these water-polished pebbles lend themselves to surreal, painterly effects. Here, a sense of the sea is captured by mosaic "waves" of grey and white washing up against a golden beach.*

opposite *In a magical example of a designer working in empathy with nature, flowing bands of earth-toned aggregates define the contours of a narrow sloping site to create a landscape of burnt serenity.*

previous page *The smooth pale paving of this country-garden terrace creates a perfect stage for a collection of abundantly planted containers.*

The effects of sunlight, rain and fluctuating temperatures demand a high quality of materials and workmanship if the appearance and function of the courtyard are to be maintained over many years. The selection of materials will make or mar a courtyard design, so it is important to make a sympathetic choice that blends with the surroundings, achieving a seamless connection with adjacent buildings and features. Choosing materials that are out of character or that attract too much attention will result in hard landscaping that is overstated, false or pretentious.

Floors are especially vulnerable because they must withstand traffic from walking, the weight of containers and furniture, and perhaps the rigours of children's games and equipment. Ground frosts and tree roots are further factors that have to be taken into consideration when choosing a flooring material. Good preparation for laying paths and terraces, including thorough groundwork, is therefore vital, because they may settle into an uneven surface or develop unsightly cracks if they have insufficient or poorly laid foundations.

Texture, one of the most versatile elements in garden design, comes into its own in the choice of materials for paving and floors, playing both a visual and a functional role. Textural possibilities range from smoothly sawn sandstone through bricks and rough granite setts to washed beach pebbles. Generally speaking, expanses of polished marble and granite look out of place in a domestic scheme and are best confined to decorative mosaic insets. Tiles and bricks are available in a huge range of colours and densities, ranging from mellow terracotta flagstones for Mediterranean themes to hard, black engineering bricks, excellent for detailing in modern designs.

floors and surfaces gallery

▼ **Ceramic tiles** are available in a huge range of shapes and sizes. There is also a wide choice of colours and textures available. Ceramic tiles are suitable for creating elaborate patterns and designs. Courtyard floors need to be laid with tough, specifically manufactured tiles and a frost-proof specification is required for all exterior work.

▲ **Aggregates** are formed from small particles of stone, glass, metal or shell. They are available in a wide range of textures and colours. They are useful as decorative mulches and surface finishes, especially in areas that are not often visited on foot. They can also be used as a smart, moisture-retaining top-dressing for containers.

▲ **Bricks** are available in a wide range of colours and textures, and can be laid in interesting geometric patterns, including herringbone and basket weave. Very hard engineering bricks are the most suitable for paving work, although old bricks can look sympathetic in rustic schemes for low-traffic paths and decorative detailing.

▼ **Crushed slate** is an attractive, though unstable, material that is best used for areas of the courtyard with low traffic. However, the crunching sound that slate makes underfoot is very satisfying. Its appearance lends itself to decorative schemes involving "dry-river bed" effects and Eastern-style surface finishes.

▲ **Granite setts** are the perfect material for building hard-wearing, slip-resistant paths. Versatile, because of their small size, they are also effective as edgings and for providing contrasting details. They are particularly useful for curved and circular formats if you are planning a fluid design of beds and borders. They can be used successfully in both formal and country-style courtyards.

▲ **York stone paving** is one of the most popular choices of flooring material for a courtyard because of its soft colour and texture, although it is rather an expensive choice. The smooth-sawn finish is elegant and practical, lending itself to both period and contemporary designs. It is also available with a riven surface, which works especially well where an aged effect is desired.

▼ **Mosaic flooring** is mainly used for highlighting a terrace, a path or the base of a formal pool. Attractive and unusual designs can be easily created with small pieces of ceramic, glass or marble tile. These are available in a range of colours and textures and can be arranged in any number of ways to create different patterns, from formal to fantastical.

▲ **Railway sleepers (ties)** and reclaimed beams make durable components in country-style schemes. They combine well with gravel if you are building a rustic path and can be easily assembled to create a flight of steps. Railway sleepers can also be used to make strong retaining walls for raised beds, ideal for growing vegetables.

▲ **Wooden decking** has become very fashionable in recent years, although users find that it can become slippery in climates with a frequent rainfall. It provides a neat solution to changes of levels and raised paths, although for safety it is important to scrub off algae regularly and fix steel mesh on steps and other high-risk areas.

▼ **Pebble mosaic** relies on tone, texture and shape for its effect. It is a popular choice for creating highlights and focal points in paths. The informal and random shape of pebbles lends itself especially well to the creation of flowing, spiral patterns. It looks particularly good in association with water features.

▲ **Gravel** is a versatile, fine-textured material, which is especially useful for filling in awkward spaces and complex shapes, as is the case with this paving and timber bridge. Gravel is relatively cheap, which means that it is an economical choice for covering large areas of courtyard as well as for finishing around planting. It is available in a wide range of grades and colours.

▲ **Slate paving** from African sources is becoming increasingly popular in dynamic, contemporary design schemes. Its rich tones and colours, and hard texture, give it a lively feeling. However, it can seem much more congenial when subtle, darker-toned details are incorporated into the design. Slate also has a ringing quality as you walk on it.

boundaries and screens

above left *This double-panel screen is partially constructed from a solid triangular section, while a staggered view can be seen through the diamond-shaped bamboo trellis below.*
above right *A neutral backdrop can be important to the success of a minimalist design. Dark grey paint reduces the visual impact of this metal fence, allowing it to fade anonymously into the distance.*
opposite *It is important to prevent a boundary from making the courtyard feel claustrophobic. This slatted screen allows for the passage of light and air.*

A courtyard depends heavily on its boundaries for enclosure and for their role in scene-setting. Privacy is important, especially in an urban situation, but avoid making walls so high that the courtyard becomes too shady or claustrophobic. The usual hard-landscaping rules apply in relation to matching materials to their surroundings, although more flexibility can be allowed in the case of wooden trellis and screening.

Existing walls are a bonus because they provide a sense of maturity. Brick and stone look wonderful in their natural state, but stylish effects can also be achieved with cheaper blockwork when it is rendered with cement and painted. Walls constructed of concrete, poured on site, are effective in a modern design; curved forms and special shapes are possible, while added colours or special aggregates make distinctive finishes.

Trellis panels can be applied direct to walls for decoration or to support plants. They make a useful device to give extra height and privacy to a low wall, and are especially pretty when covered with vines or flowering climbers. It is often desirable to enclose the courtyard completely in foliage, and, although swathes of climbers and wall plants are the obvious option, a clipped evergreen hedge is more suitable for a formal design.

A fence is perhaps the easiest option for a new boundary, being both fairly cheap and simple to install. Where formality is desired, clad fences in trellis and paint them in a discreet colour, like soft grey-green. Close-boarded or feather-edged fences make a good solid screen, but where a partially obscured view is desired, a design of open slats can be effective. Informal wattle hurdles and reed screens work best in country-style courtyards.

Metals bring a sharp, sophisticated look, best suited to city courtyards. Corrugated metal has an edgy, urban feel, while stainless steel might be used in a minimalist scheme. At the other extreme, traditional wrought-iron railings and screens look most at home with a classical-style period building.

boundaries and screens gallery

▼ **Reed fencing** panels are excellent for creating a sophisticated, although pleasantly informal, boundary screen. The fine material appears light and unobtrusive, lending itself to both Eastern- and Mediterranean-style courtyards and planting schemes. This natural material is also suitable for a country-style courtyard, perhaps surrounding a small potager.

▲ **Brick walls** have an enduring quality that lends distinction and maturity to the courtyard. They readily absorb heat, making them especially suitable for growing tender climbers and espaliered fruits such as peaches and nectarines. These can be trained on horizontal wires that are tensioned between wall bolts.

▲ **A corrugated metal panel** can be obtained in differing profiles. Although it is a distinctly industrial material, this sophisticated, fine-grooved version looks elegant and refined, producing a visual echo of the markings of the adjacent foliage. It would provide a suitable boundary or screen in a contemporary courtyard.

▼ **A "moon" window** is a clever way of providing visual relief in a solid wall, allowing a focused view to the courtyard scene beyond. Round and oval shapes work well, but this rectangle is easy to construct and provides a suitably angular foil to the soft grassy planting around it.

▲ **Trellis panels** incorporated with a solid background, such as a painted wooden fence, are very effective at creating a decorative boundary enclosure that ensures privacy and seclusion. Standing out brilliantly against its dark green setting, this reflective version employs shiny steel slats, which have been woven into a delicate-looking diamond pattern.

▲ **Wattle hurdles** are hand-woven from willow or hazel wood. They have a relaxed, informal quality that blends particularly well with soft annuals, flowering herbaceous perennials and vegetable potagers. Wattle hurdles are ideal for a country-style courtyard or perhaps to screen off or divide a vegetable plot from the rest of a larger country courtyard.

▼ **Lath screens** made from thin, narrow strips of wood can be used to create divisions or to obscure parts of the courtyard that you wish to hide from view. They can also be used on top of a rendered wall, rather like a piece of trellis. A lath screen is a good method of creating a boundary that gives a sense of privacy, without becoming claustrophobic.

▲ **Iron railings** evoke an atmosphere of grandeur and elegance, which is especially suitable for town courtyards and period buildings. They may be cast in elaborate panels or, like the example shown here, hand-forged into a low, dividing screen. For a softer effect, the railings can be covered with a climber such as clematis.

▲ **Wooden fencing** provides a lightweight, inexpensive and easily erected method of screening undesirable views and creating boundaries. This purpose-built, close-boarded fence screen uses natural wooden slats set vertically. It is elegantly finished with horizontal boards at the top and bottom.

▼ **Rendered walls** provide a clean, smooth finish over a blockwork construction. By tinting the mix, instead of painting the surface, it is made virtually maintenance-free. This pale shade is understated, creating a sheer backdrop to show off the strong forms of architectural planting.

▲ **Trelliswork screens** can be constructed from pieces of wood that are nailed together to create a lattice-work effect. The robust, square-slatted format shown here creates a strong presence that belies the sense of visual transparency. You can also buy ready-made panels in different shapes and styles. Set into the ground, trellis is ideal for training roses, clematis and honeysuckle.

▲ **Hedges** of evergreen shrubs such as this manicured *Chamaecyparis* provide fast-growing screens that are refreshingly verdant all year round. They provide a softer, more organic boundary than walls and fences. Although they are useful for courtyards, it should be noted that they need plenty of space to expand and tend to rob adjacent planting of water and nutrients.

decorative structures

There are many ways of bringing three-dimensional interest and exciting features into your courtyard. It is possible to introduce or enhance changes of level, even in a small courtyard. For example, a raised wooden viewing terrace can be constructed above a level site, and raised beds can be created with retaining walls.

Even an unpromisingly poky city space with awkward steps and basement areas can be transformed with a little reorganization. In fact, many period town houses were built with a drawing room above ground level, resulting in sub-ground areas close to the building and the main garden above. By altering the external layout, it is possible to create handsome terraces accessed by integrated flights of steps. With the clever use of retaining walls, high-level planting beds can double as screens to form a private corner, while an upper terrace can be transformed by excavating a formal pool. Conversely, a dramatic focal point can be created on a flat space, with a raised pool and fountain surrounded by a seating ledge. A naturally sloping site might lend itself to an informal treatment with a path and wood-edged steps cut into the bank.

Three-dimensional structures are easy to install and give height and interest to a level site. At its simplest, the versatile obelisk makes an eye-catching focal point alone; combined in one or more pairs, they bring instant sophistication to a formal design. A pergola, cantilevered from the house, will convert a patio into a shady dining terrace, especially luscious when laden with grape vines. Alternatively, the pergola could be constructed along a boundary, cloister-style, and draped with elegant wisteria to shade a bench. A pretty, jasmine-covered seating arbour makes an inviting resting point in a country-style courtyard or a calming retreat when framed with tall, rustling bamboos. All these structures must be robust and firmly fixed in order to carry the heavy weight of woody climbers and to withstand winds and storms.

above left *Potagers can be funky, too. Painted steel strips form a heavy basket-weave edging for a raised bed.*
above right *Containers make it possible to vary the effects of formal planting in many ways. A trough of topiary, over a wide expanse of crushed slate, suggests an aqueduct or canal suspended over a riverbed.*
opposite *Openings should reveal their secrets gradually, tempting the visitor to explore. This immaculately woven, double willow wall is entered through a willow-leaf-shaped opening, offering a glimpse of the glinting screen beyond.*

decorative structures gallery

▼ **A wooden arbour** is one of the easiest ways to introduce architectural structure to even the smallest of courtyards. This arbour is made up of trellis panels, then painted with a decorative outdoor stain to tone with the bench. You can buy ready-made trellis panels in different shapes and sizes, which can be built up into an arbour.

▲ **Timber raised beds** can be created on any level site. This highly unusual example is constructed from tall timber logs which have been painted a bold Mediterranean blue. This creates a dramatic contrast in colour with the simple planting of green, cream and grey grasses. A selection of herbs and vegetables could also be grown in the bed.

▲ **Wooden steps** built from solid sections of hardwood are one of the simplest ways to deal with a change of level. They are usually used within informal or rustic schemes, creating a natural look in keeping with a rural courtyard. Here, however, they have been cleverly incorporated with stone and concrete in an unusual modern design.

▼ **Metal obelisks** can make instant focal points that add a three-dimensional interest to the courtyard border. More sophisticated than a twig tripod and permanently enduring, a metal obelisk can stand alone as a visually light and airy structure, or become a stylish frame for training clematis or sweet peas.

▲ **Wooden pergolas** need bold sections for both strength and visual appeal. Joints must be sound and supporting posts fixed in concrete to withstand wind and the weight of plants. Hardwood is the best choice of material because it needs no further protection. Softwood should be finished with a tinted preservative stain, rather than paint, which needs regular maintenance.

▲ **Stone and wood pergolas** create a dramatic architectural presence and are suited to larger, formal courtyards. The tall, classical columns are often best left unadorned by any foliage, but such a design would be a perfect host for a cascading wisteria, allowing its pendulous racemes of flowers to dangle down through the canopy of horizontal wooden beams.

▼ **Steps inlaid with mosaic tiles** as a surface finish can be used to reinforce an Islamic theme or to give an exotic look to a modern design. It produces an eye-catching effect that can become overpowering, but with care it can be combined with other similarly finished features, such as the base of a pool, a focal point in paving or a table top and planters.

▲ **Decorative fabric screens** can be used as ephemeral sculptures for a limited season during the summer. Designs can be made from stitched or glued appliqué, or painted with waterproof dyes. Fabric screens can be used to provide privacy and shade for a seating area, or perhaps to mark a pathway or entrance for a party or social event.

▲ **Formal pools** imbue a courtyard with a sense of calm and tranquillity, looking most comfortable in a formal, classical setting. The pool can be sunk into the ground, allowing its lines to flow smoothly with the courtyard, or set above the surface within retaining walls, where the top capping can serve as a seat.

▼ **Box-style arbours** make interesting focal points in a courtyard space. They can be used to provide a niche for displaying potted plants or perhaps to house a sheltered viewing bench. This arbour is distinguished by a tiled roof that gives it a strong identity and presence, contrasting with the delicate, painted trellis sides.

▲ **Perspex (Plexiglas) screens** make an excellent windbreak or safety barrier for a pool. Lightweight and easy to fix between wooden posts, Perspex is also shatterproof (perhaps a consideration if you have young children). Translucent, coloured options are available, although this clear example, using appliquéd skeletal leaves for decoration, allows full exposure to the view beyond.

▲ **Wooden summerhouses** are luxurious hideaways that can double up as a studio, workshop or potting shed, thus providing a peaceful retreat in which to work or relax. A stylish wooden bench distinguishes this veranda-style version, creating an airy resting place, sheltered from sun and showers, and allowing the sitter to view the courtyard.

decorative effects

There are various surfaces and objects in the courtyard, many of which need or can be given different treatments, from a coat of paint or stain to a mosaic, engraved or weathered finish. Whatever job you are doing, make sure that the surface is prepared first and always follow any manufacturer's instructions.

The walls of the courtyard are perhaps the largest possible area for treatment. They can be painted with smooth or textured masonry paint, which is available in a limited range of ready-mixed colours, though many suppliers will also mix colours specially. If you are painting only a small area or simply adding some decorative detailing to a wall, then you can tint white paint with artists' colour.

Garden doors and furniture are usually made from smooth-planed wood, which can be primed and painted with exterior gloss or treated with a woodstain or varnish that is specially formulated for use outdoors. Outdoor buildings and structures, such as sheds, summerhouses, gazebos and arbours, are usually pre-treated with a preservative that can then be given a fine, decorative paint finish. After preparing the surface thoroughly, you will need to apply a coat of exterior primer, followed by an undercoat, before applying the exterior gloss paint. Be sure to allow sufficient drying time between the coats. Woodstains and varnish will allow the grain of the wood to show through and are usually applied directly to clean, dry wood.

Most fencing and trellis are made from rough-sawn wood, usually treated with a brown preservative. For a more attractive finish, use one of the new outdoor wood paints, which are quick and easy to apply, or one of the preservative stains that are available in a range of excellent colours.

Metal gates and railings can be painted with exterior gloss paint. You will need to treat previously painted metal with a rust cure and prime any new or bare metal with a metal primer before applying the top coat. It is advisable to remove any loose rust first with a wire brush.

above Appliquéd tropical fish, finished in the dappled hues of the ocean, swim across a patio wall to reinforce a deep-sea theme. **opposite** The combined colours of red- and blue-painted concrete surfaces create an exotic look, which is echoed by the planting. However, the rectangular format, reinforced by the vertical slats of the red-stained screen, stops the eye and creates a calmer, more restrained impression.

decorative effects gallery

▼ **Painted metal** must first be galvanized in order to prevent rust, after which a special outdoor lacquer can be applied by brush or, for a drip-free finish, by spraying. Factory-applied powder coatings can be used to give a smart, glossy finish to galvanized steel, but this is economical only for large projects like gates or railings.

▲ **Coloured finishes** can be used on wooden structures such as furniture. Oil-based paints are the conventional choice, although regular repainting is necessary. New water-based colours for outdoor use tend to be matt. Oil-based preservative stains are also available in a range of colours, and need no further maintenance after the first treatment.

▲ **Painting a wall** is a quick solution for a makeover or special effect. Masonry paint can be applied directly to bricks, blocks or render, and, although the basic colours are limited, bright pigments can be added to achieve more vivid results. Small, highlight designs may be added with exterior oil paints over a base coat, to avoid the trouble of special mixings.

▼ **A roughcast render** of cement and aggregates can be applied when a rusticated effect is required over a wall that has been built inexpensively using blockwork or construction bricks. This may be coloured with a surface covering of masonry paint; alternatively, tinting pigments can be integrated with the mix.

▲ **Engraving stone** brings an interesting texture to pieces of sculpture such as this magnificent Welsh-slate plaque, which is decorated with a series of elegant numerals. Chiselled and hammered effects can also be applied to other hard stones such as granite to finish the edges of steps and plinths or to create motifs in table tops or stepping stones.

▲ **Flaking paint** is usually the result of years of weathering, as in the case of this terracotta jar. However, you can achieve a similar result by applying layers of different coloured washes, interior oils or acrylics over unstable surfaces such as untreated wood and unsealed clay tiles and pots. The resulting finish will give the object a convincing aura of age and venerability.

▼ **Weathered metals** such as zinc and rusted iron have a mellow quality that blends well with plants and the outdoor environment in general. Structures such as obelisks and arbours look sympathetic in a country-style design, while containers fit well into a modern setting. This contemporary metal sculpture creates an airy effect as it spirals into the distance.

▲ **Mosaic patterns** can introduce life and character to walls in an entrance or in a shady corner. Designs can be made from any combination of glass or ceramic tiles. Ready-cut tiles are available, or fragments of colourful broken chinaware can be recycled into gypsy-style designs, perhaps highlighted with glass pebbles or beads.

▲ **A mosaic table top** adds a real air of glamour to a courtyard setting. This subtle, feminine design is made from cut-glass tiles in a range of subdued colours, including pale blue and pale green, which look charming as they reflect the light. More solid effects can be achieved using ceramic tiles, with the grouting toned to match the tile colour.

▼ **Perspex (Plexiglas)** is an unbreakable material that can be transparent, translucent or opaque, ideal for screens and windowpanes. Available in many jewel-like colours, it can add a touch of brilliance to a modern design. Here, a charmingly naïve decoration has been added with cut-out paper flowers.

▲ **Verdigris copper** is a pleasantly varied blue-green surface effect, resulting from oxidization through exposure to air and moisture. Old cooking vessels that can be turned into planters are a good source of the material, while builders' yards supply water pipes that can be transformed into informal sculpture or sheet material for facing planting containers or table surfaces.

▲ **Painted wooden decking** makes a sophisticated alternative to the usual natural brown, giving the design a sharper, more architectural look. Preservative stains are the most hard-wearing and also give the most maintenance-free finish. The dense effect of this decked stage is achieved by using three coats of a deep-toned blue stain.

Plants are the *raison d'être* of a garden. They can shape the design, create mood and change through the seasons to provide constant interest. This directory does not set out to be exhaustive but, instead, is designed to help you select the best plants for the style of your courtyard. It focuses upon all the important aspects of gardening in a restricted space, giving plenty of examples of plants for architectural structure and container cultivation as well as for covering walls and providing colour and texture throughout the year. It lists plants chosen for their style as well as their reliability in a confined space.

plant
FOCUS

architectural and specimen plants

Good planting design depends on creating a strong framework. Whether organized formally or in flowing groups, trees, shrubs and foliage perennials make up the structure of the planting. There is an array of forms and habits, leaf types and textures, so take time to work out the look you are after.

Cercis canadensis 'Forest Pansy'
Eastern redbud

A deciduous tree grown mainly for its heart-shaped leaves – a rich plum-purple in this cultivar – but gradually achieving a graceful outline with maturity. In autumn, the leaves turn a rich yellow before falling.
Height and spread: to 10m (33ft).
Hardiness: Hardy/Z 5–9.
Cultivation: Grow in fertile, well-drained soil in sun or light shade. Young trees need staking for the first three years.

Chamaerops humilis
Dwarf fan palm

For warm courtyards only, this Mediterranean palm suckers from the base, making a bushy plant, well clothed with exotic-looking leaves of glossy green. Since it tolerates shade, it makes a good choice for a courtyard garden. It is sometimes grown as a houseplant or conservatory (sunroom) plant in cold climates, where it makes an impressive specimen.
Height: 3m (10ft); spread: 2m (6ft).
Hardiness: Half hardy/Z 9–10.
Cultivation: Grow in fertile, well-drained soil in sun or light shade.

Cordyline australis
Cabbage palm

Often seen as a street tree in warm areas, the cabbage palm is a tree of pleasing outline, having a straight trunk with a symmetrical head of blade-like leaves, the central ones stiffly erect, the outer ones splaying outward and downward. Dying leaves at the base of the crown, which can look rather unsightly, should be removed. Some selections have coloured leaves.
Height: 3m (10ft); spread: 1m (3ft), sometimes more in both directions.
Hardiness: Half hardy/Z 9.
Cultivation: Grow in fertile, well-drained soil in sun or light shade.

Dicksonia antarctica
Tree fern

These are definitely the plants of the moment, dramatic as single specimens but also impressive when grown in groups. They bring an exotic feel to most schemes. They like leafy soil in a sheltered, ideally lightly shaded spot. In cold areas, you will need to pack the dormant crowns with straw or some other dry material in winter, as protection against frost.
Height: 2m (6ft); spread: 4m (13ft).
Hardiness: Half hardy/Z 10.
Cultivation: Grow in fertile soil, preferably enriched with leaf mould, in dappled shade.

Euphorbia characias 'Lambrook Gold'

This shrubby euphorbia is a variable plant distinguished by its domed heads of lime-green flowers that last for a long period over late spring and early summer. 'Lambrook Gold' has particularly vivid flowers. Those of 'John Tomlinson' are even more pronouncedly yellowish. Unnamed seedlings may not be so distinguished. Cut the stems down to the base after flowering.

Height and spread: 1.5m (5ft).
Hardiness: Borderline hardy/Z 7–10.
Cultivation: Grow in well-drained soil, preferably in full sun, though this euphorbia tolerates light shade.

Fatsia japonica
Japanese aralia

Commonly grown as houseplants, fatsias are hardy enough for outdoor use in most areas, their large, hand-like leaves giving a tropical, jungle look to any planting.
Height and spread: 3m (10ft).
Hardiness: Borderline hardy/Z 8–10.
Cultivation: Grow in any well-drained soil in sun or shade. Prune in spring, as necessary.

Festuca glauca
Blue fescue

These tufty grasses, steely blue in colour, have a variety of uses. Grow them as a low border edging, in groups or as specimens in pots. Look for varieties such as 'Harz' or 'Blaufuchs', which have strongly coloured leaves. The summer flowers are an added bonus.
Height and spread: 30cm (12in).
Hardiness: Hardy/Z 4–8.
Cultivation: Grow in any well-drained soil, preferably in sun.

Cercis canadensis 'Forest Pansy'   *Dicksonia antarctica*

Festuca glauca

Melianthus major
Honey bush
This is one of the most handsome of all foliage plants, with divided, soft silvery-grey leaves. It is best grown against a wall in cold areas. Although shrubby, it behaves more like a herbaceous perennial in cold districts. Protect from hard frosts with dry straw or bracken over winter. It is ideal for giving height to an "exotic" planting of cannas, dahlias and half hardy annuals.
Height: 2.5m (8ft); spread: 2m (6ft).
Hardiness: Half hardy/Z 9–10.
Cultivation: Grow in any fertile, well-drained soil in sun. In cold areas, a dry mulch in winter can help it survive frosts.

Miscanthus sinensis
These elegant grasses have arching leaves and plumes of brownish-yellow flowers that give a fountain effect in the courtyard. The selection 'Gracillimus', sometimes referred to as maiden grass, is especially fine, with slender leaves that curl pleasingly at the tips. Possibly even more eye-catching is 'Zebrinus', with narrow green leaves, banded horizontally with yellow, and silky brown flowers.
Height: 1.5m (5ft); spread: 60cm (2ft).
Hardiness: Hardy/Z 5–10.

Cultivation: Grow in any soil that does not become waterlogged or in a very dry site, in sun.

Musa basjoo
Japanese banana
Banana palms are generally grown in gardens for their exotic-looking, paddle-shaped, fresh green leaves, since away from the tropics any fruit that is produced is unlikely to ripen. However, the leaves alone create a tropical atmosphere.
Height and spread: 1.5m (5ft), or more in favourable conditions.
Hardiness: Borderline hardy/Z 9–10.
Cultivation: Grow in any fertile soil in full sun. In cold areas, pack loosely with dry straw over winter, as protection against frost.

Olea europaea
Olive
The European olive is gaining in popularity as a garden plant, though it is unlikely to fruit in cold climates. It naturally assumes a pleasing shape – usually dome-headed – and the grey-green leaves are attractive. An olive is ideal for a container and makes a fine feature in a Mediterranean planting scheme. In frost-prone areas, some winter protection is necessary.
Height and spread: to 10m (33ft), but usually much less in cultivation.

Hardiness: Borderline hardy/Z 8.
Cultivation: Grow in fertile, well-drained soil in full sun.

Ophiopogon planiscapus 'Nigrescens'
This diminutive plant is not actually a grass, though it looks very much like one with its firm, strap-like leaves. The colour is the main point of interest – the closest there is in the plant world to a true black, and bound to be a talking point. It looks good in a gravel garden or against white marble chippings, which provide a contrast. It spreads slowly.
Height and spread: 20cm (8in).
Hardiness: Hardy/Z 6.
Cultivation: Grow in fertile soil, preferably lime-free or slightly acid, in sun or light shade.

Phormium tenax
New Zealand flax
Phormiums are handsome perennials with blade-like leaves that arch elegantly over. They need some winter protection in cold areas and benefit from division every few years or so – they can develop brown patches if congested. 'Purpureum' is a selected form with bronze-purple leaves. The leaves of 'Variegatum' are margined with creamy white.

Height and spread: 2m (6ft) or more.
Hardiness: Borderline hardy/Z 9–10.
Cultivation: Grow in reliably moist soil in sun or partial shade. A dry winter mulch is advisable in cold districts. Remove damaged leaves regularly.

Phyllostachys
These elegant bamboos can serve either as specimens or as backdrops to other smaller plants, besides providing excellent screening material. They can be invasive, but their spread can be restricted either by planting them in large containers sunk in the ground or by inserting barriers around their roots. P. bambusoides, the giant timber bamboo, has thick green canes and copious, glossy dark green leaves. P. flexuosa is sometimes known as the zigzag bamboo because of its flexing, slender canes. Perhaps the smartest of all is the black bamboo, P. nigra, with canes that turn black with age – a truly dramatic plant in an Eastern-style planting.
Height and spread: 5m (16ft) or more.
Hardiness: Hardy/Z 6–10.
Cultivation: Grow in fertile, well-drained soil in sun or light shade.

Melianthus major   Miscanthus sinensis 'Zebrinus'   Olea europaea   Ophiopogon planiscapus 'Nigrescens'

climbers and wall plants

This plant group is crucial in a courtyard, where walls and boundaries play such a significant role. With a balance of evergreens, flowering shrubs and quick-growing annuals, it is possible to swathe the courtyard with colour and texture throughout the year.

Campsis radicans
Trumpet vine
Seldom seen in gardens, the soft orange-red, trumpet-like flowers of this vigorous, deciduous climber make an impressive show from late summer to autumn, though there is a lot of leaf by that time.
Height and spread: to 10m (33ft).
Hardiness: Borderline hardy/Z 5–9.
Cultivation: Grow in any fertile, well-drained soil in full sun.

Ceanothus
California lilac
Few wall shrubs match the impact of these when they are covered with their blue, scented flowers. The colours range from pale powder-blue to a rich indigo. There are both deciduous and evergreen forms, the evergreens being slightly less hardy and thus a riskier choice in a cold

district, though none is long-lived. They flower either in late spring to early summer or in late summer. Spring-flowering evergreens include 'Delight', 'Italian Skies' and 'Puget Blue', all with rich blue flowers.
Height and spread: to 2m (6ft), or sometimes more.
Hardiness: Borderline hardy/Z 7–9.
Cultivation: Grow in any fertile, well-drained soil in full sun. Prune after flowering if necessary.

Chaenomeles
Ornamental quince, japonica
It is possible to train these somewhat intractable, thorny plants tight against a wall, but it is easier to tie them loosely to it and allow the stems to billow forward more informally. The cup-shaped flowers, which appear either before or at the same time as the leaves unfurl in spring, are charming. C. speciosa 'Geisha Girl' has apricot flowers and a neater habit than most. The hybrid group C. × superba includes a number of worthwhile selections in red, white and pink. Among the reds, 'Knap Hill Scarlet' is perhaps one of the best. 'Crimson and Gold' has the added attraction of vivid yellow stamens.

Height and spread: 1.5m (5ft).
Hardiness: Hardy/Z 5–9.
Cultivation: Grow in fertile, well-drained soil in sun or light shade, but chaenomeles will tolerate most soils other than waterlogged ones.

Clematis
It is possible to have a species or hybrid in flower during virtually every season of the year. Best known are the summer-flowering hybrids, with their large, flat flowers, usually in vivid colours. They include 'Warsaw Nike', with rich velvety purple flowers, and 'Marie Boisselot', an excellent white variety. No clematis is truly blue, most having a touch of mauve, but one of the best in this range is 'Perle d'Azur'. For a container, try 'Sho-un', with large blue flowers over a long period.

The species have daintier flowers, though some are rampant growers. This makes them suitable for screening a large area (although only C. armandii is evergreen). Among the species, the early spring-flowering C. alpina is elegant, with its nodding, bell-like flowers (selections are available in blue, pink and white). Evergreen C. armandii has leathery leaves, unique in the genus, and

fragrant white flowers in spring. Also scented, but to a varying degree, are selections of C. montana, of which 'Alexander' has white flowers.

For later interest, C. tangutica and C. 'Bill Mackenzie' bear small, yellow, lantern-like flowers in late summer to autumn. C. 'Pagoda', another late flowerer, has dainty, pinkish-red flowers with unusually back-curved petals.
Height and spread: to 10m (33ft) (most species); to 3m (10ft) (hybrids and C. alpina).
Hardiness: Hardy/Z 4–9.
Cultivation: Grow in most fertile, well-drained soils, preferably alkaline. Site in sun or (ideally) partial shade, making sure the roots are in shade. Pruning requirements vary with the different types; refer to a specialist guide for details.

Hedera
Ivy
The ivies, all self-clinging, will bring green to even the most inhospitable parts of a courtyard, and there is more variety in leaf shape and colour than you might imagine.
H. algeriensis is a large-leaved species from the Canary Isles, usually grown in one of its variegated forms such

Campsis radicans

Clematis 'Marie Boisselot'

Clematis 'Pagoda'

Hedera helix 'Cavendishii'

as 'Gloire de Marengo', whose green leaves are irregularly margined with cream (deepening to yellow as they mature). It needs a fairly sheltered spot. The smaller-leaved *H. helix* is tougher, in fact virtually indestructible. 'Cavendishii' has creamy yellow leaf margins. 'Green Ripple' is vigorous, with distinctive, jagged-edged leaves.
Height and spread: to 4m (13ft) (*H. algeriensis* 'Gloire de Marengo'); to 45cm–8m (18in–25ft) (*H. helix* cultivars).
Hardiness: Borderline hardy/Z 8–9 (*H. algeriensis* 'Gloire de Marengo'); hardy/Z 5 (*H. helix* cultivars).
Cultivation: Grow in almost any soil, but preferably alkaline; variegated forms need some sun for the best leaf colour, while plain-leaved varieties do well in shade.

Humulus lupulus 'Aureus'
Golden hop

This herbaceous climber is a prodigious grower. Dying back in winter, once established it will cover a wall or a pergola each year, making it useful where a seasonal curtain of foliage is needed. It is pointless trying to train it, apart from in its initial stages – just let the twining stems loosely support the yellow-green leaves.
Height and spread: to 6m (20ft).
Hardiness: Hardy/Z 6–9.

Cultivation: Grow in any reasonably fertile, well-drained soil, in full sun for the best leaf colour.

Passiflora caerulea
Passion flower

Most passion flowers are hothouse plants, but the species described is reliably hardy in a sheltered spot in cold areas. The distinctive summer flowers, white with a central boss of violet filaments, are striking, and are sometimes followed by yellow, theoretically edible, fruits. The selected form 'Constance Elliot' is a real stunner, however, with fragrant, creamy white flowers. Passion flowers climb using coiled tendrils.
Height and spread: to 3m (10ft).
Hardiness: Borderline hardy/Z 8–10.
Cultivation: Grow in any fertile, well-drained soil in full sun. Protect in winter in cold districts.

Pyracantha
Firethorn

Among the toughest of garden plants, the firethorns make ideal screening plants. They froth over with creamy white flowers in early summer, which develop into clusters of orange, yellow or red berries in autumn. They are magnificent trained against a wall, but beware of planting them too near a walkway, as the stems are armed with

barbarous spines. 'Orange Glow' has vibrant orange berries, while those of 'Soleil d'Or' are golden yellow.
Height and spread: 1.5m (5ft), more if wall-trained.
Hardiness: Hardy/Z 6–9.
Cultivation: Grow in almost any soil, in sun or moderate shade.

Rosa
Rose

Few flowers can match the rose for pure, old-fashioned charm, and the climbing forms are an excellent choice when space is limited. The following are all tried and tested. 'Madame Alfred Carrière', with an abundance of rather untidy but sweetly scented creamy white flowers in summer, is especially versatile, lighting up a wall, clambering through a mature tree or swathing a sturdy pergola or arch. 'Félicité Perpétue' has dainty, crumpled flowers that open pink and fade to blush white. 'Gloire de Dijon' is early flowering and needs the shelter of a warm wall in frost-prone districts; it has large, bun-like, creamy apricot blooms. 'Constance Spry' has double, rich pink flowers.
Height and spread: to 5m (16ft) or more, depending on the variety.
Hardiness: Hardy/Z 4–9.
Cultivation: Grow in very fertile, well-drained soil in sun or light shade.

Solanum jasminoides 'Album'
Potato vine

Preferring a sheltered spot, this real beauty is an airy plant, with white flowers, each with a yellow "beak", over a long period in summer. Tie the thin stems to their support.
Height and spread: 3m (10ft).
Hardiness: Half hardy/Z 8–10.
Cultivation: Grow in any well-drained soil in full sun. In cold areas, protect with a dry mulch over winter.

Wisteria

Mature specimens of wisteria are a sight to behold in late spring, when the fragrant flowers emerge. Wisterias usually flower best in full sun, at least in cold climates. The plant is hardy, but the wood needs a good roasting to ensure flower production, hence the value of pinning the main stems to a sunny wall. In late summer, cut back any wayward new growth. Garden plants are usually selections of either *W. floribunda*, the Japanese wisteria (with violet flowers, though white and purple forms are available), or its similar but more vigorous cousin, *W. sinensis*, the Chinese wisteria.
Height and spread: to 9m (28ft).
Hardiness: Hardy/Z 4–10.
Cultivation: Grow in any well-drained soil, preferably not too rich, in sun or light dappled shade.

***Humulus lupulus* 'Aureus'**

Passiflora caerulea

***Rosa* 'Constance Spry'**

Wisteria sinensis

plants for containers

Container planting enables you to alter the courtyard through the year. Instant architectural effects and focal points can be achieved with clipped topiary and large specimen shrubs. Seasonal flowers bring a fresh look every few months and the colour schemes can be varied. They make the most impact when arranged in groups.

Agave americana
Century plant

Huge succulents with rosettes of leathery, waxy-coated leaves with toothed edges. The flower spikes can be spectacular, but generally result in the death of the central rosette. Fresh rosettes developing around the base should then be removed and grown on until they too reach flowering size. 'Marginata' has leaves edged with creamy yellow, a variegation reversed on 'Mediopicta', where the yellow appears as a broad central band. Height and spread: 2m (6ft).
Hardiness: Tender/Z 9–10.
Cultivation: Use standard cactus potting mix and site in full sun. You will need to provide some winter protection in cold areas.

Anemone coronaria
Windflower

The flowers of anemones are a welcome sight, appearing from late spring to early summer, depending on when they are planted. Planting a few pots at the same time creates a spectacular display. There are two main hybrid groups. The St Bridgid Group has double flowers, with colours varying from red, pink, violet-blue to white, while the De Caen Group has single flowers in white, red, pink, mauve or blue.
Height: 30–40cm (12–15in); spread: 15cm (6in).
Hardiness: Hardy/Z 8–10.
Cultivation: Use soil-based potting mix and keep in a sunny spot.

Buxus sempervirens
Box

This is one of the most versatile of all evergreen shrubs, very tolerant of clipping, making it an ideal topiary plant. Old, straggly plants will regenerate even if cut back hard. 'Suffruticosa' is a dwarf with tiny leaves – and very slow growing. New plants can be raised from cuttings.
Height: 1m (3ft); spread: 1.5m (5ft) ('Suffruticosa'); height and spread: to 5m (16ft) (other cultivars).

Hardiness: Hardy/Z 6–9.
Cultivation: Use soil-based potting mix and site in sun or light shade.

Eucomis autumnalis
Pineapple plant

This plant has pineapple-like flowers, with a tuft of green leaves at the top. Thriving in pots, it does best in a sheltered spot. E. autumnalis produces pale green or white flower spikes from late summer to early autumn.
Height: 20–30cm (8–12in); spread: 60–75cm (24–30in).
Hardiness: Borderline hardy/Z 8–10.
Cultivation: Grow in moderately fertile, well-drained soil in full sun. Protect in winter with a dry material such as straw.

Hyacinthus
Hyacinth

These fragrant, spring-flowering bulbs are ideal for growing in containers, but be wary of frost damage where the soil is allowed to get too wet. All cultivars, which are available in a range of bright, cheerful colours – including blue, white, pink and yellow – are bred from H. orientalis. Some spectacular cultivars include 'Amethyst' (lilac); 'Ben Nevis' (white); 'Blue Jacket'

(dark blue); 'City of Haarlem' (yellow); 'Hollyhock' (crimson); 'Pink Pearl' (rose-pink); and 'Woodstock' (deep pink).
Height: 30–60cm (1–2ft); spread: 20cm (8in).
Hardiness: Hardy/Z 6–9.
Cultivation: Use soil-based potting mix in containers, with extra grit to ensure good drainage.

Ilex aquifolium
Holly

The hollies are tolerant evergreens, usually (though not invariably) with spiny leaves. Though they can eventually grow into trees (albeit slowly), they can be clipped quite hard and are useful for simple topiary. Some selections have variegated leaves, either creamy white or bright yellow. Note that only female forms will berry, and most need to be grown in the vicinity of an accommodating male. 'J.C. van Tol' and a few others are self-fertile.
Height and spread: to 3m (10ft), but depends on the form and/or pruning.
Hardiness: Hardy/Z 6–9.
Cultivation: Use soil-based potting mix and place in sun or shade.

Agave americana

Anemone coronaria 'The Governor'

Buxus sempervirens

Eucomis autumnalis

Laurus nobilis
Bay
The laurel of classical literature, and a plant rich in associations. Bay can be grown either as a tree or a shrub and is one of the most handsome of evergreens, with its stiff, matt green leaves with crinkled edges. It can be clipped to shape (best as a ball or cone). Stems thrown on a fire or barbecue crackle satisfyingly.
Height and spread: to 3m (10ft), or less, depending on pruning.
Hardiness: Borderline hardy/Z 8–10.
Cultivation: Use soil-based potting mix and place in sun or shade.

Phormium
New Zealand flax
These grassy plants make imposing mounds of arching, sword-like leaves. There are a number of forms with coloured foliage. P. tenax 'Nanum Purpureum' is a dwarf form, useful for small gardens, with leaves overlaid with bronze-purple. The hybrid P. 'Maori Sunrise' has slender leaves striped with apricot-pink and edged with bronze. Tall flower spikes sometimes appear in summer.
Height and spread: to 2m (6ft); dwarf forms generally within 1m (3ft) or less.
Hardiness: Borderline hardy/Z 8–10.

Cultivation: Use standard potting mix and place in sun or light shade. Some winter protection may be necessary in very cold areas. Keep well watered when in growth.

Pieris
Lily-of-the-valley bush
Pieris are woodland shrubs and so do best in a lightly shaded position on the patio. Attractive as the bell-like spring flowers are, most are grown for the impact of their foliage, which is generally most striking as the new growth appears in spring. P. japonica 'Flaming Silver' has bright red new growth, margined with a pink that rapidly fades to silvery white. 'Blush' has pink flower buds that open white but retain a pinkish cast. 'Valley Valentine' is unusual, with deep purple-red flowers opening from crimson buds.
Height and spread: 2m (6ft).
Hardiness: Borderline hardy/Z 7–9.
Cultivation: Use ericaceous (acid) potting mix, ideally with added leaf mould. Place in a lightly shaded position.

Trachelospermum jasminoides
Star jasmine, confederate jasmine
An evergreen climber with curious, twisted, divinely scented, white

flowers over a long period in summer. It combines splendidly with bougainvillea in warm climates or large conservatories (sunrooms). More or less hardy, in cold areas some form of winter protection in the early years is advisable. It can be slow to get going but is rewarding.
Height and spread: to 9m (28ft).
Hardiness: Borderline hardy/Z 8–10.
Cultivation: Grow in soil-based potting mix in sun or light shade.

Trachycarpus fortunei
Chusan palm
The hardiest of the palms, this is a useful plant for bringing a touch of the exotic to cool courtyards. Stiff, pleated leaves can be 75cm (30in) across. On mature specimens, the bark becomes fibrous.
Height: to 3m (10ft); spread: 1.5m (5ft).
Hardiness: Borderline hardy/Z 8–10.
Cultivation: Grow in soil-based potting mix and place in sun or light shade. Shelter from strong winds in winter.

Triteleia laxa
Californian hyacinth
The delightfully delicate flowers of this corm look like crocuses. T. laxa 'Koningin Fabiola' bears mauve-blue flowers in summer.
Height: to 25cm (10in); spread: 8–10cm (3–4in).

Hardiness: Frost hardy/Z 6–10.
Cultivation: Grow in soil-based potting mix, and stand in a sunny sheltered spot.

Washingtonia filifera
Desert fan palm
This palm is similar to Trachycarpus but with a more open habit – leaf stalks can be 1.5m (5ft) long or even more on mature specimens – and a trunk swollen at the base. As the lower leaves die back, a "thatch" develops on the trunk, which can be a fire risk if not removed.
Height: 3m (10ft); spread: 1.5m (5ft), or more in either direction.
Hardiness: Tender/Z 9–10.
Cultivation: Use soil-based potting mix with added leaf mould and sharp sand, and place in full sun.

Yucca filamentosa
Adam's needle
This bold foliage plant, with its firm, blade-like leaves, has spikes of white flowers (usually in late summer to autumn, but not necessarily every year). Yuccas create a symmetrical effect in a container.
Height and spread: 1m (3ft) (height to 2m/6ft when in flower).
Hardiness: Hardy/Z 5–10.
Cultivation: Use soil-based potting mix, and place in full sun or light shade.

Hyacinthus orientalis 'Woodstock'   **Laurus nobilis**   **Phormium tenax cultivar**   **Triteleia laxa 'Koningin Fabiola'**

plants for scent

Scent brings an element of magic to the courtyard. Try planting herbs such as thyme and lavender close to paths where their fragrance will be released as you pass by. Different scents create different moods: the scents of roses and honeysuckle suggest a morning in the country, while the heady perfumes of lilies and tobacco plants can transform a sunny courtyard into a sultry paradise.

Brugmansia × candida
Angels' trumpets, datura
Beautiful but deadly: all parts of this plant are poisonous. The huge, trumpet-like flowers are unique. Hanging down from among the stems from summer to autumn, at night they give off an intoxicating fragrance. In a warm climate, brugmansias can be trained as spectacular standards. Selected forms have white, soft yellow or apricot flowers.
Height and spread: 1.5m (5ft) or more.
Hardiness: Tender/Z 10.
Cultivation: Grow in fertile, well-drained soil in full sun.

Choisya ternata
Mexican orange blossom
This evergreen shrub has aromatic leaves and scented white flowers in late spring. With a bun-like habit, it is ideal for providing a topiary effect without pruning. 'Sundance' has bright yellow-green leaves.
Height and spread: 2m (6ft).
Hardiness: Hardy/Z 8–10.
Cultivation: Grow in fertile, well-drained soil. Choisyas tolerate some shade and are good against a wall, but flower best in full sun.

Jasminum
Jasmine
The jasmines have a sweet scent that epitomizes summer for some gardeners. In cold areas, the most recommended species is J. officinale. It is best trained against a warm wall but is worth trying over a pergola if winter temperatures drop only a little below freezing. J. polyanthum, which flowers in late winter, is suitable for frost-free courtyards only.
Height and spread: to 3m (10ft).
Hardiness: Borderline hardy/Z 7–10 (J. officinale); tender/Z 9–10 (J. polyanthum).
Cultivation: Grow in well-drained, fertile soil in sun or part shade.

Lathyrus odoratus
Sweet pea
Annual sweet peas are mostly climbers, though some compact strains have been bred for use as border plants. Choose carefully among the varieties, since not all are scented to the same degree. Flower colours include white, pink, lavender, orange and red. Try training them on obelisks to give height to a border. Pick or dead-head the flowers regularly to encourage more flowers.
Height and spread: to 2m (6ft).
Hardiness: Hardy/Z 1–11.
Cultivation: Grow in any soil in full sun. Sow from late autumn to early spring.

Lavandula
Lavender
The lavenders are woody herbs, traditionally grown for their aromatic foliage and always associated with cottage gardens. When in flower in summer, the plants will be alive with bees. They can quickly become untidy and benefit from clipping in spring and late summer; replace straggly old plants with new ones, which are easily raised from cuttings. So-called English lavender, L. angustifolia, has a number of

excellent forms. 'Hidcote' has deep blue flowers; 'Nana Alba' is compact, with white flowers; and 'Vera' is robust, with broader leaves and lavender flowers. Slightly less hardy is the species grown commercially for the production of lavender oil – L. stoechas. This has distinctive flowers, with upswept bracts at the top of each flower spike.
Height and spread: 45cm (18in).
Hardiness: Hardy/Z 6–9 (L. stoechas Z 7–9).
Cultivation: Grow in very well-drained soil in full sun. Lavender does well in poor, gravelly ground.

Lilium
Lily
The aristocrats among bulbs, lilies have an undeserved reputation for being difficult to grow – the problem is merely that cultivation needs differ among the many species. Hybrids are usually unscented (though current breeding programmes may change that). Fragrant species include L. candidum, the Madonna lily, with trumpet-shaped, white flowers of virginal purity. L. formosanum is also white, but has strong purple flushes on the outside of the flowers, and

Lathyrus odoratus

Jasminum officinale

Lavandula stoechas

Lilium regale

L. regale has richly scented, waxy white flowers, again flushed purple outside. All the lilies are summer flowering.
Height: to 60cm (2ft).
Hardiness: Hardy/Z 4–9.
Cultivation: Lilies like cool soil but need their heads in the sun. Good drainage is essential. *L. candidum* does well in alkaline soil; *L. formosanum* needs moist, acid soil; *L. regale* tolerates most soils that are well drained. Plant lily bulbs deep, apart from *L. candidum*, which should be set just below ground level.

Lonicera periclymenum
Honeysuckle
While honeysuckles are renowned for their scent, it is worth bearing in mind when making a selection that not all species are scented. *L. periclymenum* is one of the best for fragrance, with the added bonus of early- and late-flowering forms. 'Belgica', sometimes called the early Dutch, has pink and red flowers in early summer. 'Serotina', the late Dutch, has purple and red flowers from midsummer to autumn. With their vigorous twining stems, honeysuckles are useful for covering a pergola to make a scented arbour, or for growing through a tree. With patience, they can be trained as standards.

Height and spread: to 4m (13ft).
Hardiness: Hardy/Z 5–9.
Cultivation: Honeysuckles will do well in any soil that is not too dry, as long as the roots are in shade.

Matthiola
Stock
Most stocks can be treated as annuals or as biennials, depending on the time of sowing. The white, pink, lavender or crimson flowers are an invaluable scented addition to almost any planting scheme. Brompton stocks are biennials; selected strains include double forms and dwarfs. As their name suggests, Ten Week Series will flower ten weeks after sowing, so staggering the sowing can result in a long season. *M. longipetala* subsp. *bicornis* are night-scented.
Height: 30cm (12in); spread: 20cm (8in).
Hardiness: Hardy/Z 6.
Cultivation: Grow in any soil in full sun. Sow seed from summer onward for flowers the following year and from late winter for flowers the same year.

Nicotiana × *sanderae*
Tobacco plant
On a hot day, the flowers close and droop from the stems. As the temperature drops at dusk, they

perk up to release an incense-like fragrance. Some seed mixtures produce flowers in a range of colours (white, pink and red), but there are also single-colour selections available. Dwarf varieties are excellent in a restricted space.
Height: 30–45cm (12–18in); spread: 25cm (10in).
Hardiness: Half hardy/Z 7.
Cultivation: Grow in any soil in sun or light shade. Sow seed in a propagator in early spring.

Pittosporum tobira
The pittosporums are generally grown for their foliage, but this species has clusters of sweetly scented white flowers in late spring to early summer. It is ideal in a sheltered spot, and a hedge of it is a delight in a frost-free climate. Elsewhere, it is worth trying in a container, if it can be given winter protection.
Height: 2m (6ft); spread: 1.5m (5ft).
Hardiness: Borderline hardy/Z 8–10.
Cultivation: Grow in fertile, well-drained soil in sun or light shade. It can be pruned in early spring.

Rosa
Rose
There is a wide variation in the scent of roses, with some having none at all, while others have fresh,

spicy or deep, musk-like odours. The climber 'Louise Odier' is valued for its late season (it starts flowering in midsummer) and the charm of its strongly scented, double, bright pink flowers. 'Zéphirine Drouhin', also climbing, with magenta flowers, has a warmer fragrance. The Bourbon shrub rose 'Alba Semiplena' has very fragrant, milky white flowers, while *R. xanthina* 'Canary Bird', one of the earliest roses to flower, has scented, canary-yellow flowers.
Height and spread: to 3m (10ft) (climbers); 1–2m (3–6ft) (bush types).
Hardiness: Hardy/Z 4–9.
Cultivation: Grow in fertile, well-drained soil, ideally in full sun (partial shade is tolerated but may reduce flowering). Prune in early spring, if necessary. Dead-head in summer.

Rosmarinus officinalis
Rosemary
The leaves of this Mediterranean sub-shrub are aromatic, especially in hot dry weather. Rosemary is attractive enough for use with ornamental plants; it can become leggy, but responds well to clipping and makes a good low hedge.
Height: to 2m (6ft); spread: 1m (3ft).
Hardiness: Hardy/Z 7–9.
Cultivation: Grow in free-draining, light soil in full sun. Clip over after flowering, as necessary.

Rosa 'Alba Semiplena'

Rosa 'Louise Odier'

Rosa xanthina 'Canary Bird'

Rosmarinus officinalis

plants for sun and shade

Whatever the aspect of your garden, respect your plants' needs and select them to suit the prevailing conditions. Although it can seem that all the interesting plants need sun, it is mainly flowering species that fall into this category. Flowering climbers will bloom high up, a benefit that can be enjoyed from above, while handsome foliage perennials such as hostas and ferns look wonderful in a shady bed or cluster of large containers.

SUN

Canna × generalis

These exotic-looking plants have lustrous upright leaves, often overlaid with bronze. The flowers are available in a range of colours, including red, white, yellow, orange and salmon, and appear from late summer to autumn. Like dahlias, they can be lifted and overwintered in cold areas.
Height: to 1m (3ft), sometimes more; spread: 50cm (20in).
Hardiness: Half hardy/Z 7–10.
Cultivation: Grow in fertile soil in full sun.

Cistus

These Mediterranean shrubs have sticky, aromatic stems and an easy succession of crinkled, papery flowers in summer. C. × aguilarii 'Maculatus' has white flowers, blotched blackish maroon at the centre, and C. × pulverulentus has rich cerise flowers. Cistus do well in large rockeries and on banks – where the good drainage they need is guaranteed.
Height and spread: 1m (3ft).
Hardiness: Borderline hardy/Z 7–9.
Cultivation: Grow in very well-drained soil in sun; cistus do well on poor, gravelly soils.

Convolvulus cneorum

This beautiful plant is related to bindweed, a weed in most gardens. The silvery grey leaves alone would make it worth growing, so the clear white flowers are an added bonus when they appear in summer. It revels in hot, dry conditions and, like many silver-leaved plants, looks its best in gravel.
Height and spread: 60cm (2ft).
Hardiness: Hardy/Z 8–10.
Cultivation: Grow in very well-drained soil, preferably gritty, in full sun.

Cosmos bipinnatus

With one of the longest flowering seasons of any annual, cosmos are of unquestioned value. Apart from the distinction of the glistening flowers and feathery foliage, they are excellent for cutting. They make a fine show planted en masse.
Height: to 1m (3ft); spread: 45cm (18in).
Hardiness: Half hardy/Z 9.
Cultivation: Grow in any soil in sun. Seed can be sown in situ after all danger of frost has passed.

Cynara cardunculus
Cardoon

A dramatic perennial, for use either as a specimen or in imposing groups at the back of a large border, if you have enough space. It has huge, jagged-edged leaves of silvery grey and, in summer, large, thistle-like flowers at the tops of sturdy stems.
Height: 2m (6ft); spread: 1.2m (4ft).
Hardiness: Half hardy/Z 9–10.
Cultivation: Grow in well-drained soil in full sun.

Eccremocarpus scaber
Chilean glory vine

This climber is often grown from seed as an annual, but in fact often behaves as a perennial, producing feathery foliage each year and a succession of bright orange tubular flowers until well into autumn or at least until the first frosts. It looks especially effective when allowed to scramble freely through an evergreen hedge.
Height: 3m (10ft); spread: 1m (3ft).
Hardiness: Borderline hardy/Z 9–10.
Cultivation: Grow in well-drained soil in sun.

Tropaeolum majus
Nasturtium

These are among the easiest annuals to grow, since their large seeds can simply be pressed into the ground in spring. The species encompasses vigorous trailing plants that can be used in hanging baskets or trained as climbers, as well as compact forms for filling in around other plants or growing in the cracks in paving. Flower colours include red, orange, yellow and cream.
Height and spread: to 3m (10ft) (trailing forms); other strains often within 30cm (12in).
Hardiness: Half hardy/Z 8.
Cultivation: Grow in any well-drained, preferably poor, soil in full sun.

Cistus × pulverulentus

Convolvulus cneorum

Cosmos bipinnatus

Tropaeolum majus

SHADE

Alchemilla mollis
Lady's mantle
This tolerant plant will grow as happily in full sun as in shade. In fact, in some gardens it is too happy, seeding itself with abandon in borders, tubs and between the cracks in paving. To prevent this, be sure to cut the masses of frothy lime green flowers (useful in flower arrangements) before they fade. The felted, pleated leaves hold raindrops in a most appealing way.
Height and spread: 50cm (20in).
Hardiness: Hardy/Z 4–8.
Cultivation: Grow in any soil in most light conditions.

Anemone × hybrida
Japanese anemone
These wiry perennials are excellent for bringing elegance and a spring-like freshness to the late summer garden, with their white or pink flowers. They will spread to form large clumps in time. They are ravishing in the dappled light beneath deciduous trees.
Height: 1.5m (5ft); spread: 60cm (2ft).
Hardiness: Hardy/Z 6–8.
Cultivation: Grow in moisture-retentive soil in shade or sun; lighter, drier soils are also tolerated.

Cyrtomium
Less dainty than some other ferns, cyrtomiums are especially useful for providing a strong contrast to the more flamboyant plants in the courtyard border. C. fortunei has upright fronds, while C. falcatum, which is known as the Japanese holly fern on account of its leaf shape, makes a good houseplant, although it can also be grown outdoors in sheltered areas.
Height and spread: 60cm (2ft).
Hardiness: Hardy/Z 6–9 (C. fortunei); borderline hardy/Z 7–9 (C. falcatum).
Cultivation: Grow in fertile, moist but well-drained soil in any degree of shade.

Dryopteris
Buckler fern
The dryopteris are robust ferns, invaluable for providing clumps of trouble-free greenery among other plants. D. filix-mas, the male fern, is technically deciduous, but usually does not die back completely in autumn. D. erythrosora is best in a moist, sheltered site. Its triangular fronds are glossy coppery pink when young.
Height and spread: 60cm (2ft).
Hardiness: Hardy/Z 4–8 (D. filix-mas); hardy/Z 5–9 (D. erythrosora).
Cultivation: Grow in fertile soil in shade.

Hosta
The hostas gradually increase in size each year until they make striking mounds. Unfortunately, they are like caviar to slugs, so some measure of pest control is essential. They have delicate flower spikes, but are grown mainly for their foliage. H. sieboldiana 'Frances Williams' is an old variety, with puckered, thick, glaucous green leaves, margined with creamy beige. H. sieboldiana var. elegans has thickly puckered, glaucous, bluish-green leaves and almost white flowers.
Height and spread: to 60cm (2ft) or more, depending on the variety.
Hardiness: Hardy/Z 4–9.
Cultivation: Grow in fertile, humus-rich, reliably moist soil in shade.

Impatiens hybrids
Busy Lizzies
These are among the few bedding plants that will flower profusely in shade, making them invaluable for bringing colour to shady areas. They are difficult to raise from seed, so it is easiest to buy them as bedding plants or as "plugs" in early spring. The colour range includes white, pink, red, purple and orange.
Height and spread: to 30cm (12in).
Hardiness: Tender/Z 10.
Cultivation: Grow in any soil, as long as it is not waterlogged, in light to deep shade.

Nicotiana Domino Series
Annual tobacco plants can be grown in sun but tend to wilt in hot weather, so it is better to place them in shade. The scent seems to be given off in puffs at evening time. Flowers vary in colour and can be white, pink, red or green. Single-colour strains are available.
Height and spread: 30cm (12in).
Hardiness: Half hardy/Z 7.
Cultivation: Grow in any but waterlogged soil in light shade.

Osmunda regalis
Royal fern
This deciduous fern has upright fronds. A native to bog areas, it is effective at the water's edge.
Height and spread: 1–2m (3–6ft).
Hardiness: Hardy/Z 3–9.
Cultivation: Grow in moist, preferably acid soil in light shade.

Polystichum
Although these evergreen ferns are at home almost anywhere, they are at their best in cool semi-shade. P. munitum, the sword fern, has shining green fronds. P. setiferum Acutilobum Group has elegant fronds.
Height and spread: 1m (3ft).
Hardiness: Hardy/Z 4–9.
Cultivation: Grow in humus-rich, preferably alkaline, soil in light to deep shade.

Cyrtomium fortunei

Hosta sieboldiana var. elegans

Nicotiana Domino Series

Polystichum setiferum Acutilobum Group

plants for seasonal effect

Such enormous pleasure is to be gained from the changing seasons that it would be a tragedy to ignore the potential of deciduous shrubs and perennials in favour of a design based on evergreen form. Such optimism is felt as early bulbs break the dark days of winter. Summer flowers open in quick succession, followed by a rich display of autumn leaves, which drop once more to reveal a tracery of skeletal branches.

SPRING

Anemone blanda

These bulbs provide carpets of daisy-like flowers from early to mid-spring. They are often sold as mixed colours (white, pink and blue), but single-colour selections include 'White Splendour', with white flowers, and 'Atrocaerulea', a clear blue. While they will grow in light shade, they flower best in full sun.
Height and spread: 15cm (6in).
Hardiness: Hardy/Z 6–9.
Cultivation: Grow in any soil (as long as it is not waterlogged), in sun or partial shade. Flowering is more prolific in sun.

Camellia japonica, C. × williamsii

Spring-flowering camellias are generally forms of C. japonica or the hybrid group C. × williamsii (there is no immediately apparent difference between the two). Flower colours are restricted to white, pink and red, but there is a huge variety of flower forms, including single, double and peony-form, which can make choosing among them difficult. C. 'Spring Festival', with dainty, pale pink, double flowers, is especially charming – the young leaves are faintly touched with bronze.
Height and spread: to 3m (10ft), depending on the variety.
Hardiness: Hardy/Z 7–9.
Cultivation: Grow in lime-free soil, in sun, but with some shelter from hot sun.

Crocus

With their goblet-like flowers, crocuses are among the most reliable of the spring bulbs. Most of the sturdy garden varieties are grouped under C. chrysanthus or C. vernus. C. 'Advance' is yellow and violet, C. 'Ladykiller' white and purple', and C. 'Jeanne d'Arc' pure white. C. sieberi 'Bowles' White' is

another good white, with a gold throat. Impressive when planted in drifts of one or more colours, they are also excellent for shallow bowls and troughs.
Height: 8cm (3in); spread: 5cm (2in).
Hardiness: Hardy/Z 3–8.
Cultivation: Grow in any but waterlogged soil in sun.

Erica carnea
Heath

Usually associated with winter interest, the heaths also encompass a number of spring-flowering forms that are ideal for providing tough mats of colour, although they should be kept away from plants of a clearer hue, such as most of the spring bulbs. They are excellent with dwarf conifers or in containers, and most will flower for six to eight weeks. 'Ann Sparkes' has rose-pink flowers deepening to lilac-pink and bronze-tipped foliage.
Height: 15cm (6in); spread: 45cm (18in).
Hardiness: Hardy/Z 5–8.
Cultivation: Grow in well-drained, acid or mildly alkaline soil. They prefer an open, sunny spot, but will tolerate some shade, and can also cope with windy sites.

Leucojum vernum
Snowflake

Looking like Tiffany lamps, the snowflakes are among the most elegant of the spring bulbs, with nodding, bell-like flowers on tall narrow stems. Each petal is delicately marked with green. They are especially effective when overhanging water.
Height: 35cm (14in); spread: 15cm (6in).
Hardiness: Hardy/Z 4–8.
Cultivation: Snowflakes like reliably moist soil in sun or light shade.

Magnolia stellata
Star magnolia

The shrubbiest of the magnolias, its slow rate of growth makes it ideal for even the smallest courtyard. The spidery white flowers open well before the leaves in early to mid-spring, but the shrub, with its elegant, airy habit, is attractive at all times.
Height: 1.2m (4ft); spread: 1.5m (5ft).
Hardiness: Hardy/Z 5–9.
Cultivation: Grow in fertile, well-drained soil in sun; in frost-prone areas some shelter from strong early morning sun at flowering time is desirable.

Anemone blanda

Crocus chrysanthus 'Blue Pearl'

Muscari armeniacum

Narcissus 'Actaea'

Muscari
Grape hyacinth

These charming bulbs are easy to grow and will spread like wildfire once settled in. *M. armeniacum* is the most commonly grown species, with dense clusters of deep purple flowers looking like tiny bunches of grapes at the top of the stems. *M. neglectum* is possibly a better choice – the blue-black flowers have white mouths – but both will increase rapidly. Daintier than *M. armeniacum* is *M. botryoides* 'Album'. It has slender racemes, 2–5cm (¾–2in) long, of scented white flowers.
Height: to 20cm (8in); spread: 5cm (2in).
Hardiness: Hardy/Z 2–9.
Cultivation: Grow in any well-drained soil in sun or light shade.

Narcissus
Daffodil

Spring would not be spring without the welcome emergence of the daffodils. The huge range of hybrid forms are usually divided into groups according to their physiology – there are daffodils with long cups, short cups, flowers in clusters, double flowers, for example – but among the most attractive are 'Thalia', which has white flowers (making a good combination with fritillaries), and 'Tête-à-Tête', a dwarf with reliable crops of bright yellow flowers. 'Actaea' is chiefly valued for its late flowering. Appearing simultaneously with the tulips to create a cheering spring display, it has glistening white petals and short orange-rimmed cups – plus a delicious fragrance. *N. cyclamineus* has golden flowers with a distinctive shape, the exaggerated petals being swept back and the long, narrow cup being reminiscent of a cyclamen. It is a parent of many spectacular dwarf hybrids, such as 'February Gold', 'Peeping Tom' and 'Jetfire'. *N.* 'Rip van Winkle' has rather lax stems for the weight of the spiky, double yellow flowers. It is an unusual but very good choice for growing in small containers on the patio.
Height: 20cm (8in) (*N. cyclamineus* and *N.* 'Rip van Winkle'); 30cm (12in) (*N.* 'Thalia'); 15cm (6in) (*N.* 'Tête-à-Tête'); 45cm (18in) (*N.* 'Actaea').
Hardiness: Hardy/Z 3–9.
Cultivation: Grow in any well-drained soil, preferably in full sun.

Prunus
Ornamental cherry

This huge genus includes some of the best-loved of all spring-flowering trees. They are all deciduous and mostly flower just before or just as the leaves appear. 'Snow Goose' has white flowers; 'Okame' is shocking pink. *P. mume* 'Beni-shidori' is a form of the Japanese apricot with deep pink flowers. The Yoshino cherry, *P.* × *yedoensis*, is a graceful tree. 'Ivensii' is a selected form with branches that spread horizontally and white flowers that open from pink buds. In a restricted space, *P.* 'Amanogawa' is a good choice, forming a pillar of semi-double, shell-pink flowers in late spring. The leaves, which are tinged with bronze when young, redden in the autumn. A possible alternative for a small courtyard garden is *P.* 'Spire', with its pale pink flowers and good autumn colour.
Height and spread: around 8m (25ft); *P.* 'Amanogawa' spreads to 4m (13ft); *P.* 'Spire' spreads to 7m (23ft).
Hardiness: Hardy/Z 6–9.
Cultivation: Grow in any moderately fertile soil in full sun; a little lime seems to suit them.

Tulipa
Tulip

One of the best known of all bulb groups, the tulip is available in a vast array of sumptuous colours. They are ideal for growing in the courtyard border, as well as in containers. The numbers of hybrid tulips – the most glamorous of the spring bulbs – run into hundreds, possibly thousands, and breeders introduce new varieties every year. Colours include white, pink, cream, red, yellow and a muddy purple, with some combining two or more colours. 'Spring Green' is creamy white, broadly striped with green. Black tulips are highly sought after, and 'Queen of Night' is one of the best, with deep purple-black flowers. 'Dreamboat' combines red, amber, yellow and greenish bronze.

The large, single, yellow flowers of 'Chopin' are streaked with red, while the leaves have attractive mottled markings. This tulip looks beautiful associated with primroses and dwarf daffodils. They are also perfect for pots, underplanted with rich blue violas. An unusual tulip is 'West Point', which has distinctive, golden yellow flowers, while an equally spectacular hybrid is 'Striped Bellona', with its stunning, red-and-yellow striped flowers.
Height: to 60cm (2ft).
Hardiness: Hardy/Z 3–8.
Cultivation: Grow in any soil (except for one that is waterlogged), and preferably a heavy one. Plant in full sun, but ensure that there is some shelter from strong winds.

Narcissus cyclamineus

Prunus 'Amanogawa'

Tulipa 'Queen of Night'

Tulipa 'Chopin'

SUMMER

Achillea filipendulina
Yarrow

Stiff stems carry flat heads of sulphur-yellow flowers in late summer. They hold their colour well and are excellent for use throughout the winter in dried flower arrangements.
Height: 1.2m (4ft); spread: 60cm (2ft).
Hardiness: Hardy/Z 4–8.
Cultivation: Grow in well-drained, but moist soil in sun.

Agapanthus
African lily

These beautiful plants produce lush clumps of large, strap-shaped leaves before the heads of trumpet-like flowers appear in late summer.
A. africanus is evergreen with deep blue flowers. *A. praecox* is also evergreen, with a later season than some of the others, well into autumn. The rather hardier hybrids include 'Loch Hope', which is robust and has deep blue flowers.
Height: 1.2m (4ft); spread: 60cm (2ft).
Hardiness: Borderline hardy/Z 7–10 (*A. africanus* and *A. praecox* are half hardy/Z 9–10).
Cultivation: Grow in fertile, reliably moist (but not boggy) soil in full sun. Protect with a dry winter mulch in cold areas.

Allium

The allium family includes edible onions as well as ornamental forms – all with an onion smell. They produce striking heads of blue, white or yellow flowers, followed by decorative seed-heads. *A. christophii* has lilac-purple flowers that glint with a metallic sheen in sunlight. *A. giganteum*, one of the tallest, has large purple flowers. *A. hollandicum* 'Purple Sensation' is shorter and a deeper purple.
Height and spread: *A. christophii*: height 60cm (2ft), spread 18cm (7in); *A. giganteum*: height 170cm (70in), spread 15cm (6in); *A. hollandicum* 'Purple Sensation': height 1m (3ft), spread 10cm (4in).
Hardiness: Hardy/Z 6 (*A. christophii* borderline hardy/Z 4–10).
Cultivation: Grow in any well-drained soil in sun, though they will tolerate some shade.

Bougainvillea

These are rampant, thorny-stemmed climbers for warm climates only. The "flowers" – actually coloured bracts – are long-lasting. *B.* × *buttiana* is a large group of hybrids with flowers in shades of white, yellow, purple or red. The species *B. glabra* has white or magenta flowers, which often have wavy edges.

Height and spread: 10m (33ft).
Hardiness: Half hardy/Z 9–10.
Cultivation: Grow in fertile, well-drained soil in full sun or light shade.

Ceanothus
California lilac

These shrubs – some evergreen – smother themselves with blue flowers with an abandon matched by no other group of plants. They are probably best tied loosely to a warm wall in cool districts. The species *C. dentatus* is spreading, with deep blue flowers. *C.* 'Burkwoodii' is brighter blue. *C.* 'Italian Skies' is also bright blue, but with more of a lateral spread. All are evergreen.
Height and spread: 1.5m (5ft).
Hardiness: Borderline hardy/Z 8–9.
Cultivation: Grow in any well-drained soil in full sun; in cold areas they are best grown as wall shrubs.

Cistus
Rock rose

These are shrubs for a Mediterranean garden, in fact, the hotter and drier it is the better. The tissue-paper flowers are fleeting, open for only a day, but there is usually a good succession of them. *C.* × *aguilarii* 'Maculatus' has white flowers with a central maroon blotch. *C. creticus* has flowers of a bright rose-pink.

Height and spread: to 1.2m (4ft).
Hardiness: Borderline hardy/Z 7–9.
Cultivation: Grow in poor, very well-drained soil, in full sun. Winter protection may be needed in very cold areas.

Cosmos atrosanguineus

The chocoholic's plant, the single, blood-crimson flowers, of velvety texture and produced over a long period from midsummer to autumn, really do smell of delicious melted chocolate. Site it near the front of a border so that you do not miss the smell.
Height: 75cm (30in); spread: 45cm (18in).
Hardiness: Borderline hardy/Z 7–9.
Cultivation: Grow in moderately fertile, well-drained soil in sun. Winter protection is advisable in cold districts.

Crocosmia 'Lucifer'

The best of the crocosmias, this robust plant has stiff, pleated leaves with large heads of brilliant flame-red flowers from midsummer. The leaves are effective in flower arrangements.
Height: 1.2m (4ft); spread: 8cm (3in).
Hardiness: Borderline hardy/Z 5–9.
Cultivation: Grow in any garden soils, in sun or light shade, but avoid sites that are too hot and dry.

Agapanthus 'Loch Hope'

Allium christophii

Bougainvillea glabra

Crocosmia 'Lucifer'

Dahlia cultivars

These plants bring colour and flamboyance to the late summer and early autumn garden. As with other heavily hybridized plant groups, new varieties are introduced each year, and the best selection is to be found in mail-order catalogues. Flowers can be huge, cactus- or waterlily-like, pompons or balls, or more diminutive, but always eye-catching in shades of white, cream, pink, yellow, orange and red. Pinch out the growing tips for bushiness and dead-head to keep the flowers coming.
Height: to 1m (3ft); spread: to 60cm (2ft), depending on the variety (dwarfs to 45cm/18in tall).
Hardiness: Half hardy/Z 9.
Cultivation: Grow in most well-drained soils, in full sun, although a rich soil is preferred. Tall varieties will need staking.

Echinops ritro 'Veitch's Blue'

This tough, rather coarse plant will be alive with bees when the star-like blue flowers open. The prickly grey-green leaves are also very attractive.
Height: 60cm (2ft); spread: 45cm (18in).
Hardiness: Hardy/Z 4–9.
Cultivation: Grow in any, even poor, soil in an open, sunny situation.

Ipomoea nil
Morning glory

This annual climber is grown for its trumpet-like flowers. They are usually in clear shades of blue, though purples and reds, as well as white, are also possible. *I. indica*, the blue dawn flower, has funnel-shaped, purple-blue flowers.
Height and spread: to 3–4m (10–13ft).
Hardiness: Tender/Z 10.
Cultivation: Grow in moderately fertile, well-drained soil in sun.

Lilium
Lily

Hybrid lilies are the easiest to grow, having been bred as border plants. 'Black Beauty' has deep red "turkscap" flowers and is one of the best for scent. 'Eros' has scented, pinkish-orange flowers, also turkscap. 'Brushmarks' is one of the many so-called Asiatic hybrids — sturdy plants with large flowers — with rich orange flowers marked with red.
Height: to 1.2m (4ft).
Hardiness: Hardy/Z 4–8.
Cultivation: Grow in well-drained soil in sun (ideally in a position where their roots are shaded).

Pelargonium

These popular plants flower prolifically all summer long, in all shades of pink, bright red and white. Use them in borders, in hanging baskets, window boxes and any kind of container, possibly alongside other tender perennials such as verbenas and felicias. There are too many hybrids to mention individually, but pelargoniums are usually classified into various groups, among which are the following. Ivy-leaved pelargoniums have thick, shield-like leaves on trailing stems, making them ideal for edging a large container. Zonal pelargoniums, a large group and for many the typical pelargonium, have leaves banded ("zoned") with a darker colour. Regal pelargoniums are upright, with large, richly coloured flowers.
Height and spread: Usually to 45cm (18in).
Hardiness: Tender/Z 10.
Cultivation: Grow in any well-drained soil in full sun. For pot plants, use any standard potting mix with added grit or perlite.

Plumbago capensis

This South African climber is grown for its appealing sky-blue flowers, produced over a long period in summer. The plant does not climb unaided, but needs to be tied to a support. In cold areas, it is often grown as a conservatory (sunroom) plant in a container, and is easily kept within bounds.

Height and spread: 1.5m (5ft), more in a favourable site.
Hardiness: Tender/Z 9.
Cultivation: Grow in well-drained soil in sun or light shade.

Salvia × sylvestris 'May Night'

The salvias are a huge genus containing many worthwhile plants. This one has tall spikes of indigo-blue flowers.
Height: 70cm (28in); spread: 45cm (18in).
Hardiness: Hardy/Z 5–9.
Cultivation: Grow in moderately fertile, well-drained soil in sun or light shade.

Thunbergia alata
Black-eyed Susan

This striking plant, which is usually grown as an annual in cold areas, is a climber that is also effectively grown in hanging baskets and allowed to trail down. The simple yellow or orange flowers have pronounced deep purple-brown throats — hence the exotic common name.
Height: to 2m (6ft); spread: 25cm (10in) (more where grown as a perennial).
Hardiness: Tender/Z 10.
Cultivation: It will tolerate most soils in sun or light shade.

Dahlia 'Claire de Lune'

Ipomoea indica

Lilium 'Eros'

Pelargonium 'Black Magic'

AUTUMN

Acer palmatum
Japanese maple

Attractive the whole time they are in leaf, acers take on a new dimension in autumn when the leaves turn yellow, red and orange. This fleeting display is likely to vary from year to year, depending on the weather. Soil type can make a difference too, with most acers producing their most vivid colour in acidic conditions. There are a vast number of selected forms, some with dainty filigree foliage.
Height and spread: 1.2–8m (4–25ft), depending on the variety.
Hardiness: Hardy/Z 5–8.
Cultivation: Grow in any soil, but preferably leafy and fertile, and with some overhead shade. Protect from strong winds and spring frosts.

Aster × frikartii
The flowers of this daisy-like perennial appear in late summer and early autumn. The dark violet-blue flowers have yellowish-orange centres. 'Mönch' has long-lasting, lavender-blue flowers.
Height: 70cm (28in); spread: 40cm (16in).
Hardiness: Hardy/Z 5–9.
Cultivation: Grow in well-drained, moderately fertile soil in full sun.

Cotoneaster
The cotoneasters are tolerant of many situations that other plants abhor. Among the best for late interest is deciduous C. horizontalis. The leaves turn a vivid red before falling at the same time as the berries ripen to red. Another good choice for late colour is evergreen, ground-covering C. cashmiriensis, with vivid red berries.
Height and spread: C. horizontalis: height 1m (3ft), spread 1.5m (5ft); C. cashmiriensis: height 30cm (12in), spread 2m (6ft).
Hardiness: Hardy/Z 5–8.
Cultivation: It will grow in most soils in sun or light shade. C. cashmiriensis tolerates deep shade.

Kniphofia
Red hot poker, torch lily

Some pokers have a long flowering season that extends well into autumn. 'Royal Standard', at 80cm (32in) tall, has flower spikes that are citron-yellow at the base and crimson at the top. 'Toffee-nosed' is an aptly named hybrid (growing to 1m/3ft tall), with cream flowers tipped with brown. Large pokers are best in isolated clumps, but smaller ones make excellent border plants.
Height: around 1m (3ft); spread: around 60cm (2ft), depending on the variety.

Hardiness: Hardy/Z 5–6 (most pokers, although some are borderline).
Cultivation: Grow in soil that does not dry out in summer while not being very wet in winter, in sun.

Parthenocissus
These foliage plants are grown for their autumn colour. Clinging by means of suckering pads, they are ideal for covering walls. P. henryana has dark green leaves marked with silver, turning red in autumn. P. tricuspidata is the well-known Boston ivy. For a change, try growing it into the branches of a deciduous tree. The selected form 'Veitchii' has leaves that open purple in spring, mature to green, then turn red-purple in autumn.
Height and spread: 10m (33ft).
Hardiness: Hardy/Z 4–9 (P. henryana is borderline hardy/Z 7–9).
Cultivation: Grow in fertile, well-drained soil in sun or partial shade.

Rudbeckia fulgida
Black-eyed Susan

This plant makes a vivid display in autumn, with yellow or orange daisy flowers, each with a black eye, above the mounds of dark green foliage.
Height: 60cm (2ft); spread: 30cm (12in).
Hardiness: Hardy/Z 4–9.
Cultivation: It will grow in most soils in sun.

Sedum spectabile
Ice plant

Above their fleshy, grey-green leaves, ice plants produce flat heads of scented, pink flowers in autumn, loved by bees and butterflies. The flowers last for a long period, gradually turning a rich brown. Selections include 'Herbstfreude' and 'Brilliant' as well as less robust white varieties.
Height and spread: 45cm (18in).
Hardiness: Hardy/Z 4–9.
Cultivation: Grow in any well-drained, even poor, soil in full sun.

Sorbus
Rowan

The rowans are good trees for the urban courtyard, casting little shade and tolerant of pollution. Most have autumn berries, which are a food source for birds. S. aucuparia 'Fastigiata' is narrowly upright, useful where space is at a premium. The berries ripen to orange in autumn as the leaves turn red or yellow. The Kashmir rowan, S. cashmiriana, has pearl-like white berries that stay on the tree after the leaves have fallen.
Height: to 10m (33ft); spread: 7m (22ft); (S. cashmiriana: height: 4m/13ft; spread: 3m/10ft).
Hardiness: Hardy/Z 5–8.
Cultivation: Grow in any well-drained soil in sun or light shade.

Aster × frikartii

Rudbeckia fulgida

Sedum 'Herbstfreude'

Sorbus cashmiriana

WINTER

Acacia

Wattle, mimosa

The acacias are pretty trees or large shrubs, with masses of fluffy, duckling-yellow flowers in late winter among the ferny grey leaves. *A. baileyana* usually makes a bigger plant than *A. dealbata*, which is a delightful choice for a sheltered courtyard. Acacias are prodigiously fast growers, but they take well to pruning and make good wall shrubs.
Height: 6m (20ft); spread 4m (13ft); less in a container or if wall-trained.
Hardiness: Half hardy/Z 8–10.
Cultivation: Grow in lime-free soil in full sun.

Clematis cirrhosa 'Freckles'

One of very few winter-flowering climbers, this clematis has nodding, bell-like, creamy white flowers, spotted with maroon, during any mild spell in winter, but is at its best as the season draws to a close. The foliage sometimes acquires bronze tints, an attractive by-product of a sudden cold snap.
Height and spread: to 6m (20ft).
Hardiness: Hardy/Z 7–9.
Cultivation: Grow in fertile, well-drained, ideally alkaline, soil in sun or light shade. Best against a sunny wall in cold areas.

Cyclamen coum

Sowbread

The hardy cyclamen is invaluable for providing ground cover (albeit not evergreen) in dry shade. The dainty flowers, with their distinctive, back-swept petals, appear from late autumn into winter and can be purple-violet, pink or white. 'Album' is a selection that produces white flowers only. The leaves are beautifully marbled.
Height: 8cm (3in); spread: 10cm (4in).
Hardiness: Hardy/Z 5–9.
Cultivation: Grow in moderately fertile, moist but well-drained soil in partial shade; drier soils are tolerated.

Galanthus

Snowdrop

Among the first of the bulbs to flower in winter, snowdrops are universally loved. *G. nivalis* is the species most usually grown, but so freely do they hybridize that there are a vast number of named forms. 'Flore Pleno' has double flowers, the petal tips touched with green. *G.* 'Atkinsii' has elongated petals and broad, grey-green leaves.
Height and spread: 10cm (4in).
Hardiness: Hardy/Z 3–9.
Cultivation: Grow in reliably moist soil, preferably where they will be shaded when dormant – beneath a deciduous tree or shrub is ideal.

Hamamelis

Witch hazel

The witch hazels would be among the first choices for a winter-flowering shrub were it not for their very specific cultivation needs. Besides their spidery, scented flowers, they have the added plus of (usually) fine autumn leaf colour. *H.* × *intermedia* 'Vesna' has pale copper-coloured flowers and outstanding autumn colour. 'Pallida' has large, sulphur-yellow flowers in mid- and late winter.
Height and spread: 4m (13ft), but slow-growing.
Hardiness: Hardy/Z 5–9.
Cultivation: Grow in rich, ideally lime-free, soil in a sunny site sheltered from strong winds.

Helleborus

Hellebore

The hellebores are long-lived plants that gradually make more and more impressive clumps. *H. niger*, the Christmas rose, produces its glistening white flowers in the very depths of winter, though it can be difficult to establish. Slightly later-flowering *H. orientalis* is easier and plants often self-seed. Flowers are subtly coloured in a predominantly dusky range of purple, pink and creamy white (sometimes the flowers are spotted with purple).

Especially desirable are the rare yellow and clear red forms.
Height and spread: 30cm (12in).
Hardiness: Hardy/Z 5–9.
Cultivation: Grow in any moist but not waterlogged (and preferably alkaline) soil in sun or shade.

Skimmia japonica 'Rubella'

The skimmias make satisfying mounds of evergreen foliage with clusters of sweetly scented flowers in late winter. On this form, the vivid pink, unopened buds are a feature.
Height and spread: 1.2m (4ft).
Hardiness: Hardy/Z 7–9.
Cultivation: Grow in fertile, well-drained soil in sun or light shade; most skimmias do best in slightly acid conditions.

Viburnum tinus

The shrubs in this genus provide interest throughout the year. Some are grown for their flowers in winter or spring, others for their berries, and some for both. *V. tinus* has white flowers in late winter and early spring, followed by bluish-black berries. 'Gwenllian' has pink-tinged, white flowers, opening from dark pink buds.
Height and spread: 3m (10ft).
Hardiness: Hardy/Z 7–9.
Cultivation: Grow in any fertile, well-drained soil in sun or light shade.

Galanthus 'Atkinsii'

Hamamelis 'Pallida'

Helleborus orientalis

Viburnum tinus 'Gwenllian'

plants for eating

Nothing can beat the flavour of home-grown produce. It is remarkably easy to grow a few vegetables and herbs, even on the tiniest of terraces. If you feel daunted by the prospect of a vegetable potager, at least fill some pots with herbs, salad leaves or tomatoes. You can even grow a small apple tree in a pot or train a grape vine on some trellis or around a pergola.

EASY VEGETABLES

Many vegetables are suitable for growing on patios and in courtyards, either in containers or raised beds, and many are extremely decorative. Some reliable varieties are listed here, but consult seed catalogues, since new varieties are introduced each year.

Aubergines/eggplants (*Solanum melongena*) have similar requirements to tomatoes but need a long growing season and are best grown under cover in cold areas. 'White Egg' has egg-shaped white fruits that hang in clusters like grapes. Other good varieties include 'Long Purple' and 'Monkeymaker'.

Cabbages (*Brassica oleracea* Capitata Group) can be grown for crops throughout the year. 'Marner Early Red' is very early, with beetroot-red leaves that can be used raw or cooked. 'Vertus' is a Savoy cabbage that has good resistance to frost. 'Castello' is a good summer cabbage.

Carrots (*Daucus carota*) can be sown in succession for cropping throughout the year. 'Flyaway' is an early maincrop variety that has been bred for resistance to carrot root fly. There are also some interesting cylindrical varieties, such as 'Amsterdam Forcing 3', 'Sweetheart' and 'Chantenay Red Cored'.

Courgettes/zucchini (*Cucurbita pepo*) should not be put outside until the last frosts have passed unless you can protect them with cloches. Courgettes are usually grown as bushes. They can be sown under glass from late spring to early summer. Harvesting should take place from mid-summer onwards. Varieties of courgette include 'Ambassador', 'Burpee Golden Zucchini', 'Early Gem' and 'Gold Rush'.

Onions (*Allium cepa*) can be grown either from seed or from "sets". Plant in autumn and spring to ensure continuity of cropping. 'Giant Zittau' is a good variety for autumn planting and keeps very well. Reliable varieties include 'Red Baron' and 'White Prince'.

Peppers (*Capsicum* species) need a long growing season in a sheltered spot. 'Bendigo' is suitable for an unheated greenhouse. Other excellent varieties include 'California Wonder', 'Delphin', 'Marconi', 'Sweet Spanish Mixed' and 'Yellow Lantern'. The related chillies include 'Hungarian Wax', with long, pointed yellow fruits, and 'Cayenne', with very hot fruits that can be used fresh or dried. Other good chilli peppers are 'Hot Gold Spike' and 'Serrano Chilli'.

Potatoes (*Solanum tuberosum*) are divided into earlies and maincrop. The tubers need to be sprouted in a light, cool, well-ventilated place prior to planting, but are sometimes sold ready-sprouted. New potatoes can be grown in large, deep tubs. 'Charlotte' is nice in salads.

Runner beans (*Phaseolus coccineus*) are grown as annuals and tolerate some shade. They can grow fairly tall, so need to be trained on a structure such as a twiggy tripod. Runner beans also have attractive flowers. Good varieties include 'Sunset' and 'Czar'.

Swiss chard (*Beta vulgaris* Cicla Group) is a highly decorative vegetable that can be used in an ornamental scheme. It has large, glossy, dark green leaves on creamy white stalks. Both parts can be eaten. Ruby chard is similar, but the stems are a brilliant red and the leaves are a deep purple-green in some varieties and green in others. You can sow Swiss and ruby chard in late spring, harvesting from late summer to the following spring. The leaves can be cut from the mature plants when you need them.

Tomatoes (*Lycopersicon esculentum*) are the ideal patio vegetable (fruit, actually), revelling in warm sunshine and thriving in large containers or growing bags. 'Tigerella' is a pretty variety with yellow-striped fruit. 'Sungella' is a heavy cropper with low acidity.

Lycopersicon esculentum

Phaseolus coccineus

Malus domestica

Prunus persica

WALL FRUITS

A sunny wall is a gift to any fruit-lover. Espaliers or cordons make the most economical use of space, and trees can be bought ready-trained. If the wall is shaded for much of the day, try the Morello cherry.

Apples (*Malus domestica*) and pears (*Pyrus communis*)

are good in cold areas, since both need low winter temperatures to trigger good flowering. Pears need a reliably warm summer and autumn for the fruit to ripen fully. Look for varieties grafted on to dwarfing rootstocks if space is at a premium.

Figs (*Ficus carica*) are ideal

patio crops since they thrive in containers. In cold areas, only the fruits that emerge right at the start of the season will ripen. Remove any small fruits that appear in mid-summer and towards the end of the growing season.

Grape vines (*Vitis vinifera*)

make handsome plants whether trained against a wall or over a pergola, and can be grown solely for ornament. For edible crops, thin the fruit trusses themselves as well as the grapes within each to produce shapely, tapering bunches.

Peaches (*Prunus persica*)

are excellent wall crops, but in cold districts the blossom will need shelter from early frosts. The related nectarines (*P. persica* var. *nectarina*) and apricots (*P. domestica*) have similar needs. In frost-prone areas, a plum can be a safer bet.

Peaches and nectarines that are fan-trained against a wall provide a decorative feature. They need a warm, sunny site; nectarines do better in warmer conditions and are less hardy.

Plums (*Prunus cultivars*) are

hardy in a range of climates and some varieties can survive cold winters. Hardy varieties can be grown in an open site, but less hardy types are best trained against a warm, sunny wall. The spring blossom should be protected from frost. Dessert plums include 'Belle de Louvain', with large purple fruits, and sweetly flavoured 'Greengage'. Cooking plums include 'Laxton's Cropper' and 'Pershore Yellow'.

HERBS AND SALAD LEAVES

Most herbs and salads can be grown in containers, making them ideal patio crops, especially since, in all probability, they will be within

arm's reach of the kitchen door. There is nothing nicer than plucking a selection of fresh herbs from outside to use in cooking.

Herbs are unlike most other

edible plants in that they do not have high nutrient requirements. For this reason they can be fed and watered like other container plants. Collections of herbs, including parsley, thyme, basil, sage, oregano and marjoram, can be grown in the side pockets of a strawberry planter. Chives (*Allium schoenoprasum*) are also suitable for growing in a container and have the added advantage of small pink flowers in the summer. Mint can be invasive, so is best confined to a container on its own, rather than grown with other plants.

Leafy vegetables suitable for

growing on the patio include all varieties of lettuce, particularly the cut-and-come-again types, which regrow after cutting ('Bionda Foglia' is a good variety). 'Little Gem' is a quick-growing dwarf that hearts quickly. Mixtures of lettuce, endive and chicory will provide a mixed salad patch. Rocket (arugula) can be sown from spring to late summer for successive crops (but is quick to run to seed in summer).

CARING FOR CROPS IN CONTAINERS

Most edible crops need to be grown in a sunny spot and they will appreciate the extra shelter and protection a patio or courtyard provides. Correct watering and feeding are essential, however, if the plants are to be productive as well as decorative.

Fruit and vegetables in containers must never be allowed to dry out, so make sure they receive regular – and thorough – waterings. Most fruits need sunshine to ripen properly, so site containers where they will get maximum benefit. From mid-summer, selectively trim back any new leafy growth to expose the ripening fruits.

Regular feeding is necessary in order to replace the nutrients that will be rapidly used up from the potting mix.

Some chemical fertilizers are formulated to suit particular crops. A tomato fertilizer, for example, can be used on most fruit crops; leafy vegetables are best fed with a high-nitrogen fertilizer. Fertilizers are best applied as a root drench. Organic gardeners should look for products based on seaweed extract.

Pyrus communis

Vitis vinifera 'Purpurea'

Allium schoenoprasum

Beta vulgaris

suppliers

UNITED KINGDOM

Anthony de Grey
Trellises
Broadhinton Yard
77a North Street
London
SW4 0HQ
Tel 020 7738 8866
Fax 020 7498 9075
www.anthonydegrey.com
Trellis

Avant Garden
info@avantgarden.co.uk
www.avantgarden.co.uk
Contact Joan Clifton
*Architectural ornaments, planters
and topiary frames*

Barbary Pots
45 Fernshaw Road
London SW10 OTN
Tel 020 7352 1053
Fax 020 7351 5504
www.barbarypots.co.uk
Containers

Chilstone
Victoria Park
Fordwood Road .
Langton Green, Tunbridge Wells
Kent TN3 0RE
Tel 01892 740866
ornaments@chilstone.com or
architectural@chilstone.com
www.greatbritain.co.uk/chilstone
also in Cheshire, tel 0161 775 6410
Sculpture

David Craig
The Mill
Mill Lane
Langley Moor
Durham DH7 8JE
Tel 0191 378 1211
Fax 0191 378 0411
www.davidcraig.co.uk
Furniture

Fairweather Sculpture
Hillside House
Starston
Norfolk
IP20 9NN
Tel 01379 852266
www.fairweathersculpture.com
Sculpture

Franchi Sementi
Seeds of Italy
Tel/fax 020 8930 2516
grow@italianingredients.com
www.seedsofitaly.com
Vegetable seeds

Garden & Security Lighting
39 Reigate Road
Hookwood
Horley
Surrey
RH6 0HL
Tel 01293 820821
Lighting

Gaze Burville
Newtonwood Workshop
Newton Valence
Alton
Hampshire
GU34 3EW
Tel 01420 587467
Furniture

Indian Ocean
Trading Company
Tel 020 8675 4808
www.indian-ocean.co.uk
Furniture

Italian Terrace
Pykards Hall
Rede
Bury St Emunds
Suffolk IP29 4AY
Tel 01284 789666
Fax 01284 789299
www.italian terrace.co.uk
Containers

Natural Driftwood Sculptures
43 Gladelands Way
Broadstone
Poole
Dorset BH18 9JB
Tel 01202 699616
Fax 01202 593270
info@driftwoodsculptures.co.uk
www.driftwoodsculptures.co.uk
Sculpture

Redwood Stone
The Stoneworks
West Horrington
Wells
Somerset BA5 3EH
Tel 01749 677777
Water features

Simon Percival
Sunnymead Works
Toadsmoor Road
Brimscombe
Gloucestershire GL5 2UF
Tel 01453 731478
www.simon-percival@
sculpt.netkonect.co.uk
Water features

Stuart Garden Architecture
Burrow Hill Farm
Wiveliscombe
Somerset
TA4 2RN
Tel 01984 667 458
Fax 01984 667455
sales@stuartgarden.com
www.stuartgarden.com
Trellis

Terre de Semences
Ripple Farm
Crundale
Canterbury
Kent CT4 7EB
Tel 01227 731815
Vegetable seeds

The Modern Garden Company
PO Box 5868
Dunmon
CM6 2FB
Tel/fax 01279 851900
www.moderngarden.co.uk
Furniture

UNITED STATES

Bear Creek Lumber
P.O. Box 669
Winthrop
WA 98862
Tel (800) 597-7191
Fax (509) 997-2040
www.bearcreeklumber.com

Gardener's Supply
Company
128 Intervale Road
Burlington VT 05401
Tel (800) 863-1700
www.gardeners.com

Garden Oaks Specialties
1921 Route 22 West
Bound Brook NJ08805
Tel (732) 356-7333
Fax (732) 356-7202
www.gardenoaks.com

High Plains Stone
P.O. Box 100
Castle Rock CO 80104
Tel (303) 791-1862
www.highplainsstone.com

Lowe's Home Improvement
Warehouse
www.lowes.com

The Home Depot
www.HomeDepot.com

AUSTRALIA

EcoScreen
Call state distributor for stockists
Decorative lattice

Haddonstone Pty Ltd
104-112 Bourke Street,
East Sydney NSW
Tel (02) 9358 6688
Stone paving and garden ornaments

North Manly Garden Centre
510-512 Pittwater Road
North Manly NSW 2100
Tel (02) 9905 5202
Fax (02) 9905 5620
Furniture, containers and sculpture

Cotswold Garden Furniture
42 Hotham Parade
Artarmon NSW 2064
Tel (02) 9906 3686
Fax (02) 9906 5417
Furniture

Mary Moodie's Pond, Pump and
Pot Shop
Southern Aquatic Garden Centre
110 Boundary Road, Mortdale
Tel (02) 9153 0503
Peakhurst Garden Centre
874 Forest Road, Peakhurst
Tel (02) 9533 4239

Diamond Valley Garden Centre
170 Yan Yean Road
Plenty Vic 3090
Tel (03) 9432 5113
Fax (03) 9432 5116

Austral Watergardens
1295 Pacific Highway
Cowan NSW 2081
Tel (02) 9985 7370
Fax (02) 9985 7024

Wagner Solar
Call 0800 064 790 for stockists
Lighting

NEW ZEALAND

Collensotree and Landscape
679 Whitford Road
RDI
Whitford
Tel (09) 530-9120
*Paving, pergolas, decks and
water features*

Exotic Earth
92 Eastdale Road
Avondale
Auckland
Tel (09) 828 6876
Outdoor garden design

Landscape Connection Ltd.
66a Bradbury Road
Howick
Auckland
Tel 0800 681 564
*Brick and blockwork,
as well as paths, patios
and decks*

index

ACKNOWLEDGEMENTS

The publisher would like to thank the following garden owners, designers and institutions for kindly allowing their gardens to be photographed for the purposes of this book. All photographs were taken by Steven Wooster, unless otherwise stated.

t = top   b = bottom   c = centre
l = left   r = right

18 Balmuir Gardens, Putney, London 134br
Mr. and Mrs. Batten, Kati Kati, New Zealand 51b; 112t
Mrs Bilboul, London 26r; 126tl; 127tl (design John Wyer at Bowles & Wyer; 3 Churchbuses, Church Lane, Berkhamsted, Hertfordshire HP4 2UB; tel 01442 877200; fax 01442 870484; admin@bowleswyer.co.uk; web www.bowleswyer.co.uk)
Bill and Amanda Alexander, Crouch Hill, London (design Lucy Summers) 69t; 159
Charlotte Gross, London (design Declan Buckley/dbdesign@dircon.co.uk) 7
Chaumont 2001 48r; 121 and 123b ('Flowing Banisters/design Gardeners of the Conservatory) 66b and 135tc ('Ribbons'/ design Sylvaine Dallot and Sabine Nebulung/ sculptor Etienne Poule); 76–77 ('L'Archipel'/ design Shodo Suzuki Japan); 84t, 85t and 123tr ('Aquatic Mosaiculture'/design Jean Louis Cura, Marc Felix and Michelle Schneider); 99t, 128 and 131tl ('The Loire, Willows and Silken Stone'/design Philippe Herlin and Daniel Jud); 102t ('Desert Sea'/design Glass Garden USA and Green & Garden, France); 107 and 131tl (Jacqueline's Garden'/design Michel Gallais, Eva Demarelatrous and Michel Arnaud); 120 ('Risseau'/design Monica Varengo and Gabrielle Gelati); 129l; 131bl
Clare Hall, Chiswick (owner and designer) 61; 135br
Declan Buckley and Bernard Hickie 47; 74; 81; 83r; 86l; 132 (design Declan Buckley/dbdesign@ dircon.co.uk and Bernard Hickie/bernard hickie@ mac.com
East Ruston Old Vicarage, Norfolk (design Alan Gray and Graham Robeson) 27l; 58–59; 122tr; 130d; 142l
Ekow Eshun 43br; 105c (design Declan Buckley/dbdesign@dircon.co.uk)
Ellerslie Flower Show 2001, New Zealand 41b ('Earth in Mind/design Sonya Findlay); 78 ('Peace Foundation') 99b ('Contemporary Cubes/design Trish Waugh); 106b ('Beach, Bush and Backyard'/ design Auckland Regional Council); 109 ('Garden Tours of South Australia'); 110r ('Welcome to Manakau'/ design Nigel Cameron)
Eric and Sue Faesenkloet, Takapuna, New Zealand (design Ted Smyth) 2–3; 44b; 112b
Forge Cottage, Jasper's Green, 135tl; 135tr (design Carolynn Blythe)
Gerad Kite, London 88–91 (all) (garden design Declan Buckley/ dbdesign@dircon.co.uk and hard landscaping by Robert Kite/Kitescape tel 020 7738 6512)
Hamilton Botanic Garden, New Zealand 65b; 76t; 123tc
Hill Spink Design 32–35 (all except 34t); 122br
Gordon and Joy Fisher, Papamoa, New Zealand 96; 113t; 123tl; 127b
Grahame Dawson and Alex Ross, Auckland, New Zealand 14; 20; 41t; 135bl
Jan and Stephen Franklin, Greenhithe, New Zealand 70–73 (all except72bl and br; 72t; 73tl and tr)
Jane Hicks, Holly House, London 50
Jennifer Diamond, London (design John Wyer at Bowles & Wyer, 3 Churchgates, Church Lane, Berkhamsted, Hertfordshire HP4 2UB; tel 01442 877200; fax 01442 870484; admin@bowleswyer.co.uk; web www.bowleswyer.co.uk) 18; 134tc)
Jenny Rogers, London 43bl; 113b and 127tr (design Declan Buckley/ dbdesign@dircon.co.uk)

Joan Clifton, London (owner and designer) 135tr; 160
John Tordoff (owner and designer) 48l; 80; 82l; 83l; 86r
Leeann Roots, London (owner and designer) 68
Little Cottage, Lymington 131b (photographer Jo Whitworth)
Michael Bowie, Auckland, New Zealand 19; 124r; 126tr; 130tr (Nigel Cameron Design)
National Garden Exhibition Centre ('The Family Garden'/design John Ketch) 84b; 134tl ('The Sensory Garden'/design Louise Burns)
Renée Lynch, London (design Sally Court) 79; 82r; 123bl; 126br; 138r; 139r
RHS Chelsea Flower Show 2001 (all photographs taken by Peter Anderson) 13 ('The Carpet Garden'/design Michael Miller and the Prince's Foundation); 22t; 25 and 102b ('Circ Contemporary Man's Garden'/design Andy Sturgeon); 49l (design Tom Stuart-Smith); 49r (design Andy Sturgeon); 85b; 72br; 104l; 126bl; 130tl ('The Sensory Garden'); 131tr ('The Garden of Tranquillity'/ design Charles Funke Associates); 104c; 156; 157 ('A Garden for Learning/design Woodford-West)
RHS Hampton Court Flower Show 2002 42; 136 ('Mercedes Benz Garden'/design Sarah Urbele); 86c ('Eastern Promise'/design Jane Rendell and Sarah Tavender); 97 and 101t ('P&O Cruises Tropical Experience'/design Jane Mooney); 101b ('Fresh Faces'/Designscape); 110l; 126b and 135b ('The Specsavers Garden'/design Lee Jackson and Naila Green); 111 ('Mitsubishi Urban Chic'/design The Courseworks Design Team); 129r ('Babylon'/design Sally Fell); 4–5; 131t ('The Paradise Garden'/design Elizabeth Apedaile)
RHS Tatton Park Flower Show 2001 52–55; 122tc; 134b ('Living Edge'/John Lewis Garden/design Butler Landscapes Design and Construction, Oaklea Cottage, Wem Lane, Prees Green, Whitchurch, Shropshire SY13 2BW, tel 01948 841079, butlerlandscapes@virgin.net); 66t ('Food for Thought/design Becky Lomas and Mark Payne); 94, 100; 122tl and endpaper ('Garden of Illusion'/ design Andy Stockton, Daniel Sterry and Adam Ash); 126tc ('The Stonemarket Garden'/ design Geoffrey Whiten); 158
Ron Sang, Auckland, New Zealand (garden design Ted Smyth/architect Rong Sang) 45, 94 (both); 105l; 133
Sir Miles Warren, Christchurch, New Zealand 31bl and br; 125
Sumil Wickes, London (design Lara Copley-Smith) 40; 46b; 82c; 87l; 122b; 123br
Susan Sharkey, Brentford (owner and designer) 23; 48c; 58t
Ted Smyth Design, Takapuna, New Zealand 114–117 (all)
The Dillon Garden, Dublin (owner and designer Helen Dillon) 21; 118; 122bl
The Heatley Garden, Takapuna, New Zealand (design Margaret Phillips and Michael Poulgrain) 16–17 (all); 24; 36; 44t; 98l; 130br
The New Art Centre Sculpture Park and Gallery, Roche Court, near Salisbury, Wiltshire 134bl ('Hermetic Numerals' by John Das Gupta)
The Puttnam Garden, London (design Verney Naylor) 60; 65t
Trevyn McDowell 38–39 (both); 127tc (design Paul Thompson)
West Green House Garden, near Hartney Wintney, Hampshire (design Marylynn Abbott) 130b

Other photographs in the book were taken by:
Andrea Jones 142cr; 143cl; 144cr; 145r; 146r; **Caroline Arber** 72bl; 139cr; **Debbie Patterson** 51t; 130tc; 134tr; **Jo Whitworth** 8 (Iford Manor, Bradford-Upon-Avon, Wiltshire); 9 (13 College Cross, Islington, London/design Diana Yakeley); 67; 124l (RHS Hampton Court Flower Show

1999/'Feng Shui Garden'/design Pamela Woods); 131br; 131b; 146cl; **Jonathan Buckley** 29b (RHS Chelsea Flower Show 1999); 34t; 62 (RHS Chelsea Flower Show 1999); 127bl; 127br; 138l; 140l; 142cl; 143l; 144l; 148l; 148cl; 148r; 149l; 149cr; 149r; 150cl; 150r; 151l; 151cl; 154cl; 155cl; 155cr; 155r; **Marie O'Hara** 151r; **Michelle Garrett** 143r; 144r; **Peter Anderson** 140cl and cr; 140r; 141cr; 145l; 145cl; 145cr; 147cl; 149cl; 151cr; 152r; 153l; 153cl; 153cr; 153r; 154l; 154cr; 154r; 155l; **Sarah Cuttle** 46t; **Simon McBride** 10; 146l; 147l; 147r; 152cr

The publisher would also like to thank the following picture agencies and photographers for allowing their images to be reproduced in this book:
Jonathan Buckley 104r (RHS Chelsea Flower Show 2001/'Circ Contemporary Man's Garden/design Andy Sturgeon); **Garden Exposures Photo Library** 22b (photographer Andrea Jones); 87r (photographer Andrea Jones/Jardin Atlantique, Paris); **Steven Wooster** 6; 11

(Chelsea Flower Show 2000 (design Brinsbury College); 12 (Michael Reed, Auckland, New Zealand); 28 (RHS Chelsea Flower Show 2000/'The Garden of Reflections'/ design Allison Armour); 31t Boardman Garden; 43t (Liz Morrow, Auckland, New Zealand); 63 Dennis Greville, Christchurch, New Zealand; 64 Mrs. Cooke, Auckland, New Zealand; 69b RHS Chelsea Flower Show 1999/The Conran Garden; 103 RHS Hampton Court Flower Show/design Bonita Bulaitis; 106t (Shirley and Terry Hooper, Auckland, New Zealand (design Nigel Cameron Design); 108 Millennium Harbour/design Michele Osborne;
The Garden Picture Library 30 (photographer Graham Rice); 98br (photographer John Glover)

The publisher would also like to thank The Chelsea Gardener (125 Sydney Street, London SW3 6NR, tel 020 7352 5656, fax 020 7352 3301) for kindly lending plants and accessories for the purposes of photography.

NOTE TO READER

Each of the plants in this section has been given a hardiness rating (for European readers) and a zone range (for readers in the United States):-

Hardiness Ratings

Frost tender Plant may be damaged by temperatures below 5°C (41°F).
Half hardy Plant can withstand temperatures down to 0°C (32°F).

Frost hardy Plant can withstand temperatures down to -5°C (23°F).
Fully hardy Plant can withstand temperatures down to -15°C (5°F).

Plant Hardiness Zones

The Agricultural Research Service of the U.S. Department of Agriculture has developed a system of plant hardiness zones. Every plant in the Plant Focus section has been given a zone range. The zones 1–11 are based on the average annual minimum temperature. In the zone range, the smaller number indicates the northern-most zone in which a plant can survive the winter and the higher number gives the most southerly area in which it will perform consistently. Bear in mind that factors such as altitude, wind exposure, proximity to water, soil type, snow, night temperature, shade and the level of water received by a plant may alter a plant's hardiness by as much as two zones.

Zone 1 Below -45°C (-50°F)
Zone 2 -45 to -40°C (-50 to -40°F)
Zone 3 -40 to -34°C (-40 to -30°F)
Zone 4 -34 to -29°C (-30 to -20°F)
Zone 5 -29 to -23°C (-20 to -10°F)
Zone 6 -23 to -18°C (-10 to 0°F)

Zone 7 -18 to -12°C (0 to 10°F)
Zone 8 -12 to -7°C (10 to 20°F)
Zone 9 -7 to -1°C (20 to 30°F)
Zone 10 -1 to -4°C (30 to 40°F)
Zone 11 Above 4°C (40°F)